SOCIAL MEDIA & THE ADOLESCENT DIGITAL TRIBE

Navigating the Teen World State

STEPHEN J SMITH

PUBLISHING INFORMATION

Copyright © 2019 A Wired Family LLC

All rights reserved.

ISBN-9780578577241

To schedule Stephen to present at your school, mental health group, business or other organizations, please email us at: marybeth@awiredfamily.org

To purchase books in quantity, please email your request to marybeth@awiredfamily.org

Follow us on social media:

Facebook - https://www.facebook.com/awiredfamily/

Twitter – @awiredfamily

For my wonderful wife and best friend Mary Beth, and our children, Beth and Jenni, grandkids Stephen, Maria, Liam, Emily, Kenzie, and son-in-law Jason.

Without your love, kindness, and support, this book would not have been possible.

Love,
Steve, Dad, Poppy

TABLE OF CONTENTS

Foreword

For some reason, you decided to buy a book on helping your child manage their online presence. Perhaps it was a discussion with another parent that brought you to this place. Or, maybe it was tiring of hearing your child clamoring for a phone or a specific app. Or, conceivably, it was one of the weekly—if not daily—news stories you heard on your drive to work, concerning how a child had misused technology, creating a family crisis.

There is no right answer to why you're here. At least you know that the judgments you make regarding technology are among today's most significant parenting decisions. I hope when you've completed this book, you'll agree with my premise.

If you are expecting this book to be a magic wand that in three quick steps provides a robust online strategy to include ironclad protection for your child and family, you should be looking in the fiction category at Amazon, Barnes & Noble, or wherever you purchased this book. Short of taking all technology out of your child's hands, there is no guarantee of protection, yet that's not necessarily the preferred solution either.

If used properly, technology can be a great thing.

Much like the automobile, digital technology is here to stay. The only change will be the various iterations and processing power it will deliver, and the content accessible by adolescent minds. So, much like a car, you just need to learn to drive—and to navigate the never-ending labyrinth of networks and apps that continue to populate what I call the Digital World States (DWS) of teens and adults.

I've attempted to keep this book entertaining, and most importantly, relevant to parents living in a digital world. So, if you're expecting writing of the engaging standard of Hemingway, F. Scott Fitzgerald, George Orwell or Aldous Huxley, you will be sorely disappointed.

But since I mentioned Aldous Huxley, author of *A Brave New World,* there are aspects of today's world that seem to summon Huxley's ghost as we already begin to see elements of his predictions coming to fruition.

In Huxley's renowned book, you'll recall "The Director" giving a tour to students while explaining the process by which humans are cultivated inside bottles and then conditioned—or as some might say, brainwashed to accept certain moral "truths."

The Director within what is called the World State, tells the students that this conditioning is known as sleep teaching, or more scientifically, "hypnopaedia."

The process instructs the citizens to believe in the value of society over the individual. People exist only to serve the nation. For society to survive, each must be both a consumer and a worker. They must buy, buy, buy—and then work, work, work. It's their job to be both consumers and workers, which in turn keeps the economy stable and robust. Buy lots of stuff. Use lots of stuff. Do your job!

The World State has a caste system of several groups.

For example, the Alphas are smart, tall, and muscular. (Just look at the young male/female anchors on cable and network news!) Others, such as the Betas, Gammas, Deltas, and Epsilons are short, dumb, fat, and ugly. (Just look at any character on the Simpsons.)

All non-Alphas are kept "stupid" by giving them substances such as alcohol and depriving them of oxygen while they are languishing inside the test tube.

In Huxley's World State, sex is much like a college fraternity pledge's dream, i.e., considered casual, non-romantic, sometimes regularly scheduled, and explicit.

"Everyone belongs to everyone else," which means a man can sleep with any woman he desires at any time.

For the woman, however, there is little choice.

Although we are a far cry from a formal caste system in the Western world, the plethora of content delivered through the programmed algorithms of social media, cable TV, streaming services and network airways have created, to some extent, a tribal belief system or what I call a Tribal World State (TWS). Each tribe preaches its moral truth through its version of hypnopedia.

Both adults and children choose information that exists within their bubble of current beliefs. Tailored feeds from the Digital World State divide us into tribes and sub-tribes.

In his book, Antisocial Media: How Facebook Disconnects Us and Undermines Democracy, Siva Vaidhyanathan looks specifically at Facebook's impact on society. However, I think much of his conjecture is just as relevant for Snapchat, Instagram, and Tik Tok.

Vaidhyanathan writes:

"Over time, Facebook not only rewards the items that are likely to generate the most markers of engagement (clicks, likes, comments, shares) but also learns to tailor the News Feed of every Facebook profile. The longer you are on Facebook, the more you engage with items on Facebook, and the more you teach Facebook to send you more of the stuff that is very much like what you have already indicated interests you. Both Facebook and Google call this a test of 'relevance'."

This test of relevance creates a homogenized stream of views, or what writer and entrepreneur Eli Pariser dubbed the "filter bubble."

Your child and their friends have their own filter bubble. It provides the walls of their Adolescent Digital Tribe (ADT). Rightly or wrongly, that bubble might also contain its moral truths which may or may not synch with that of your family.

CNN is—for some—a filter bubble. Fox News is a filter bubble. Your child's Instagram, Tik Tok, Snapchat feeds are filter bubbles –

often stoked by artificial intelligence invisibly feeding the ADT and helping to form their morals and value systems.

Today's media are unlike the days of three network TV channels delivering objective news to our homes each evening at 6:00 P.M.

Our self-serve digital content world which "celebrates diversity," in fact has created anything but diversity.

It's created a digital caste system.

The difference between the caste system in A Brave New World and today is that now, everyone believes they are the handsome, beautiful and smart Alphas, and everyone else is the short, fat, stupid and ugly Betas, Gammas, Deltas, and Epsilons.

Look, I get it. As parents, we have enough guilt to sink a battleship. Right? Many moms and dads work, shuttle kids to soccer practice, help with homework, go to PTO meetings and often try to volunteer when possible, while also trying to be good spouses, girlfriends, boyfriends, sons, daughters, uncles, aunts, and friends.

As such, I won't guilt you for the ADT your child may have entered. However, whose fault is it if they have unfettered access to social media and the world without the tools to filter out what is right and wrong? Let's be honest. It's you.

In fact, in 2007, I was yelling at the top of my lungs that the iPhone would be the next great chapter in Western education. And while I felt the technology was both captivating and galvanizing, I also didn't stop to think of its long-term consequences.

Nor did most parents. So, I'm the last one who should be pointing the finger at you.

However, as of this writing, it is nearly 2020. We've seen the good, the bad, and the ugly of such ubiquitous technology in the hands of kids. But no one can deny we have also seen a mercurial change in how kids handle stress. Anxiety and depression are on the rise among young people. The questions on the lips of the mental health professionals, teachers, counselors, school resources officers, parents, and principals are:

"Is the increase of teen depression, suicide ideation, and suicide due in part to social media and video games?"

"Is the growth of sexting due to technology, or is it a symptom of a growing cultural shift to highly sexualized media found in movies, streaming videos, and music?"

"Are video games making my child more aggressive?"

This book attempts to answer some of your questions, and perhaps cultivate further discussion with your child, spouse, extended family, friends, and your child's teachers.

In this book, you will see the results of our survey of about 2500 students aged thirteen to eighteen in Ohio, Indiana, and Kentucky, concerning their relationship to technology and how it makes them feel. We'll see the apps they're using and the time their devices are in use.

We'll see if sexting is an issue with teens, and if so, at what age.

We will also pull back the curtain on how teens feel about porn and whether they think it is an issue within their peer group, along with many other concerns.

So, sit back with an iced tea, cup of coffee or your favorite adult beverage and spend some time navigating the digital world that has helped to create the ADT of teens through their use of social media, video games and mobile technology.

ONE

The Tragedy of Not Knowing

I n 1961, there was a young boy in our neighborhood who somehow created chaos wherever he went. He destroyed furniture, painted the dining room table with Crisco oil, was evil to his siblings, broke windows, lost hundreds of dollars of toys, books, papers, and money—and blamed every indiscretion on an imaginary friend.

He was also the most dreadful student in almost every subject he took at his growing, suburban Catholic school.

His parents were exhausted dealing with him, and both he and they loathed report card time, knowing his grades would be near failing. His conduct in class and failure to be responsible littered his report card's right column with red check marks and notes, such as:

Your son does not follow directions.
Works below his abilities.
Fails to meet even the lowest expectations of our school.
Bothers others in the class.
I cannot recommend him to be an altar-boy due to his grades and behavior.

Today, such a young man generally is diagnosed as having ADHD. He most likely will be prescribed medication such as Ritalin or will receive therapy to help him deal with his condition. He will be assigned an IEP (Individualized Education Program) intended to help children reach educational goals more quickly than they otherwise would. But this was 1961. No such help existed.

I became somewhat of an expert on this condition, because I was that kid.

I mention this because there was a lot we didn't know about kids like me. Many were written off as slow, lazy, or disrespectful. Some dropped out. Others settled into low-level jobs upon graduating high school. But some were continually encouraged by exhausted but tenacious parents, and they eventually succeeded—even flourished.

In 1902, British pediatrician Sir George Still first identified what we know today as ADHD. At the time, he referred to it as hyperkinetic impulse disorder, meaning that kids like me could not control their behavior as well as other children. However, he pointed out that unlike what most teachers thought at the time, this was not a reflection on the child's intelligence.

I really wish he could have told that to Sister Mary Anne at my school back in the 1960s. She thought I was nothing short of an ill-behaved idiot who would never amount to anything.

Regardless, it took over sixty years for the medical community to recognize what became known as ADHD. Sixty years on, and we still don't know the specific cause. How many kids' lives would have been different had doctors recognized it as a real condition?

That's where we are today with technology and kids.

We don't know if the increase in depression, anxiety, self-harm, suicide ideation, and suicide are the reasons for this increase. But there are some in the medical community who believe the overuse of such technology might play a role.

For example, a 2019 article in PSYCOM, **by** Katie Hurley, LCSW suggested:

"One study out of the University of Pittsburgh, for example, found a correlation between time spent scrolling through social media apps and

negative body image feedback. Those who had spent more time on social media had 2.2 times the risk of reporting eating and body image concerns, compared to their peers who spent less time on social media. The participants who spent the most time on social media had 2.6 times the risk.[1]"

However, we are at the very beginning of such research. As we discovered with ADHD, the path is long, and many suffer until conditions are understood.

This point should be relevant to all parents and guardians of children. Lack of research and the time to understand childhood conditions can impact a whole generation of children. The overuse of social media and video games has been a concern for my wife Mary Beth, a retired 6th-grade teacher, and me since 2008. It's the reason for A Wired Family.

In July 2018, we did a one-question national survey with young women between the ages of eighteen and twenty-four and asked the following question:

Do media and social media put pressure on you to look and act a certain way?

80% of the young women said yes.

We then conducted another survey with females between the ages of thirteen to eighteen and asked the same question.

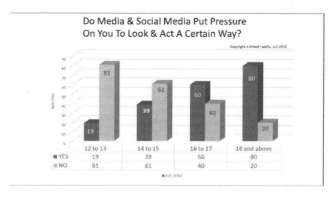

Above is a graph of the results.

As the chart indicates, as girls grow older, they become more conscious of the expectations of media and social media in terms of how they act—and specifically this means how they act as females. Within a peer group, or what I call their ADT, girls are often consumed with the one tool that escalates these feelings, i.e., Instagram.

In March of 2017, British writer Lucy Whittaker penned an article for A Wired Family, entitled Instagram and Self-Esteem. In this piece, she told the story of Essena O'Neill.

"A couple of years ago, an Australian then-teenager and ex-model named Essena O'Neill admitted to her unhealthy obsession with the app, and many young adults share the same sentiments."

"Instagram users find themselves taking ten photos before posting a so-called candid or deleting posts because of the lack of likes.

"According to The Guardian, O'Neill quit the platform, calling it "contrived perfection made to get attention.

"If this is how Instagram manipulates its older users, can you imagine how detrimental it is to our young daughters?"

It's not just that girls are comparing their bodies to those of their friends, but rather, they often scroll through and follow the accounts of celebrities—who to no surprise are generally from the Entertainment World State or (EWS.)

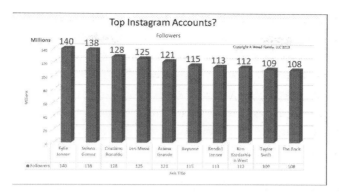

As of the time of writing in July 2019, the above Instagram accounts had the most followers.

Kylie Jenner, Selena Gomez, Ariana Grande, Beyonce, Kendall Jenner, Kim Kardashian, and Taylor Swift represent seven of the top ten Instagram accounts defined by their number of followers.

With the possible exception of Taylor Swift, each provocatively presents themselves to their followers.

For example, July 17th, 2019 at 10:56 A.M., Kylie's new photo of her breasts spilling out of a black bikini and titled: A Bikini Kind of Life had 4,747,026 likes in eleven hours.

Selena Gomez, on the other hand, deleted the app from her phone for mental health reasons.

She said:

"I used to use it a lot, but I think it's become really unhealthy for young people, including myself, to spend all of their time fixating on all of these comments and letting this stuff in."

Although Gomez still occasionally posts, she borrows a phone to post any believed to be necessary. However, about a month before she quit the app, she posted a photo of herself in what appeared to be a red bra or bikini top and received almost 12 million likes.

Kendall Jenner, who often models for Calvin Klein, posted a very revealing underwear video ad to her account. Although you might see more revealing promos during a thirty-second Victoria Secret ad, the focus on her "thigh gap" and posterior aren't exactly therapy for a teen girl follower with body issues.

However, even I must admit the video of her piloting a jet ski and then knocking off the cap of a bottle with her foot without moving the floating plastic decanter was impressive.

On July 14th, 2019, Ariana Grande posted a scantily-dressed picture of her snuggling up with equally sparsely-clad Normani. The image was followed by a photo—or a photo-shopped image—of her naked body painted in purples and blues. It certainly was artistic and well done. But again, is it healthy for young teen girls that might already be struggling with body image?

Beyonce's recent posts on Instagram seem to have been toned down from years past. Perhaps motherhood has that impact on young women? However, videos of her stage act from 2018, much like the other accounts I mentioned above, are both revealing and suggestive.

Kim Kardashian and Taylor Swift's accounts are what you might expect, with Kim K selling products along with an exposition of her breasts and butt, while Taylor Swift, almost 30 years old as of this writing, has so far avoided the over-sexualization of her brand.

Often, parents ask me about apps that I feel are the most disconcerting. I mentioned many in this book. But we can't forget the websites that children access that can change their view of the world as well. For example, I talk about Instagram and its possible impact on a young woman's body image, but of greater concern are websites such as Teen Vogue.

Teen Vogue started in 2003 as a print magazine and the little sister to the better-known Vogue. Similarly, the magazine focused on fashion and celebrities. However, its target market comprised teen and tween girls.

After a significant drop in readership in 2015, the magazine reduced its print publication and bolstered its online presence. In 2017, the print edition was shuttered and the publication became solely web-based. That all sounds well and good. However, if you're losing money, what strategy do businesses often adopt? If you answered "focus more on sex"–you're the winner.

Case-in-point: in the early 1990s, I was working for a production arm of Multimedia Entertainment and later its broadcast division. It was at this time that the now infamous Jerry Springer Show was launched. Initially, the program was shot in the downtown studios of Cincinnati's WLWT and was an issues-oriented and political talk show similar to that of the Phil Donahue program. Guests included Oliver North and Jesse Jackson, with deep, thoughtful conversations about homelessness and gun control.

However, given its poor ratings, the company threatened the show's cancellation. In an attempt to save the program, the producer was fired and a new direction was adopted. With its move to Chicago and a new focus on sex, transvestites, porn and baby-daddies, an empire was born. The program ran from 1991-2018 and Jerry Springer, who can still be seen occasionally driving in downtown Cincinnati in his Bentley, doesn't need to worry about his retirement plan.

Let me be clear. If you're an adult and you want to read more articles or watch additional videos about sex, transvestites, baby daddies and Ghi Ghi The Stripping Clown, more power to you. But in the case of Teen Vogue, their readers are not adults. They're children, kids who are exposed to very adult content, such as:

- Having Sex When You're Fat: Tips on Positions, Props, and Preparation
- How to Be an Ethical Hookup Partner
- Everything You Need to Know About Anal Sex
- Oral Sex 101: What You Need to Know About "Going Down"

Are we promoting safe sex with these articles or are we promoting the experimentation of sex among twelve, thirteen and fourteen-year-old children? Or, is the publication looking to gain readership and more profits? I think you know the answer.

As a parent, providing access to such sites is your call. Every adult has their own values and moral compass. But if these topics are "off the table" within your family, you need to be aware that such benign-sounding websites are not always what they seem to be.

By the way, does anybody else see the irony of not being able to sell a cigarette to someone under the age of eighteen, but we can publish an anal sex guide for a child? Does this seem counter intuitive? But I digress.

I know. You're a busy mom or dad and you need to cut to the chase. What does all of this mean? Why should you care?

Simply put, it took years for some very bright people to diagnose, understand, treat, and even agree on a name for a condition impacting thousands of children each year. They still don't know why the condition exists, but today, at least everyone agrees ADHD is real and at least there are now treatments.

Meanwhile, how many kids were written off during the sixty-plus years following Dr. Still's discovery? We don't know. Was the growth of ADHD due to genetics? Or was it caused by the growth of mothers smoking and drinking, or by laundry detergents, hair spray, television, radio or maybe even Twinkies?

We just don't know.

This all brings me back to my most significant concern. As a world, we often adopt technology without concern for the consequences. In fact, we give it to our kids without *understanding* the technology. This, frankly, is naive parenting.

I always tell our audience of adults that if you don't understand the technology of today, you won't stand a chance of understanding what is coming. And what is unfolding will impact you, your child, and society in general. My concern is, most parents don't understand the technology they have placed in their child's hand.

How will they grapple with artificial intelligence, facial recognition, deepfakes, virtual reality, Blockchain, and 5G? Each of these technologies will bulldoze those that haven't paid attention to the building storm called "the next decade."

We are indeed in the midst of the most significant technological sea change in the history of man. Self-driving cars, LiFT, and Uber sre changing the auto and transportation industries. But do we know the long-term impact on human fatalities due to an increase or decrease in accidents?

Here are a few other areas in which the advance of technology is potentially outpacing the human brain:

The **meat alternatives market** is exploding, with restaurant sales of such products rising 268% from 2018 to 2019.
This will change the meat industry, its processing technology, and the diet of Americans. However, there has yet to be a long-term study on how such processed foods affect the human body.

3D printing will allow industries and individuals to print anything from a new human ear, to aircraft, to cars and guns.
They will provide methods for creating products quickly, economically, and accurately. But this same technology will allow individuals to build their products without the means to study their safety or ethics.

Virtual Reality (VR) will allow anyone at any time to travel the world without leaving their couch. With its other technological cousins, i.e., Augmented and Mixed Reality, such technology will provide tremendous training and educational opportunities for both young and old. However, in 2019, all three are used for VR pornography which in some cases allows the user to be part of each sex scene. I write about this later in the book.

Blockchain is a technology for packing, storing, and transmitting data, transparently, and securely. You might think of it as a kind of account book or register that contains a list of all exchanges made between users. Without going into too much detail, it will help with the transfer of currency, securities, shares, bonds, votes, and many other things each of us does throughout the year or day.
However, with such technology, there may not be the need for intermediaries during sales and transactions. Users can conduct peer-to-peer transactions directly. This blockchain technology might threaten business such as Uber, Airbnb, eBay, Amazon, Fiverr, and others. Moreover, it will change the way currency is viewed, exchanged, and valued.

Artificial Intelligence is already used in almost every industry, from fast food to fast cars, medicine, manufacturing, and the growth of automation, agriculture, retail, and others. Most autonomous cars will use AI to gain a certain level of autonomy on the road.

Virtual assistants such as Siri and Alexa all use AI to both learn and put into context our habits, to provide relevant information to facilitators such as Apple and Amazon.

As we know, much can be learned about you and your family from the everyday conversations you have in your home. Do we trust that such virtual assistants are not recording your every word and using AI to assist for more nefarious purposes?

Will AI's use in automation eliminate factory jobs? Will it eliminate positions at fast-food restaurants? Will menial jobs be eliminated, creating even more poverty and unrest in the Western World?

What about the technologies most of us have adopted and given to our children? Do we know what physical and psychological impact social media, digital technology, Wi-Fi radio waves, 5G technology, and Blue Tooth headphones will have on the minds and bodies of this generation of children?

For example: Globally, over 300 million Blue Tooth headsets have been sold each year since 2016, but little research has been published about the impact of planting radio waves deep inside a child's ear.

Due to auto deaths in the US, laws were enacted requiring car manufacturers to install seat belts in all vehicles made after 1968. Similarly, such actions need to be taken in the technology sector. However, it took hundreds of thousands of deaths and injuries before there was a change within the auto industry.

Are we willing to take that same chance with our kids and technology? As parents, we can't wait for the government to solve all of our problems. It's up to us to be proactive and to understand and consider the possible unintended consequences of the technology we use and give to our kids. As with everything in life, there are unintended consequences.

TWO

Unintended Consequences

Allow me to provide a recent—somewhat unknown—real-life example of how changes in technology often are well ahead of society's ability to foresee possible conflicts and problems. I used this example in our first book.

Consider the story of an Indiana Farmer losing a lawsuit to Monsanto. The farmer had purchased soybean seeds developed for feeding livestock. Knowing the seeds were harvested from genetically enhanced soybean plants impervious to certain weedkillers, he decided to plant the seeds rather than feed them to livestock. He later saved the resulting soybean plants to be sold, while also harvesting some of the seeds for replanting and then growing in subsequent years.

His thinking: Why pay for a product each year if it can reproduce itself? According to the Wall Street Journal:

"The court unanimously found that farmer Vernon Bowman violated Monsanto's patent on herbicide-resistant soybean seeds by using them to grow successive generations of similarly endowed crops, rather than consuming or selling the seeds."

To put it simply, if you replace the word soybean with music, Mr. Bowman "was stealing copyrighted material." By purchasing one version of the seed and replicating it, he had somewhat created the "the agrarian version of Napster." Well. Maybe that's a stretch.

My point is that every new technology creates issues we could not have predicted.

Who would have thought the large, awkward cell phones that we see on syndicated shows like Seinfeld would have evolved into the small, powerful devices we use today to play games, communicate with friends and family and post videos on places like YouTube, Tik Tok, Instagram and Snapchat?

This evolution of technology also requires a change in parenting skills. Parenting today is a much different animal than in years past. For example, I can recall purchasing our oldest daughter a cell phone when she turned sixteen and began driving; our rationale related to safety. If there were an accident or flat tire, she'd give us a call.

Four years later, when our youngest daughter turned sixteen, text messaging had begun to grow in popularity. By 2002, text messaging became ubiquitous due in part to it being agnostic concerning wireless carriers. It allowed a user to multitask without regard to time constraints, and it was very portable. You could send a text during a movie, while in a meeting, or from the backseat of your parents' car—or, from just about anywhere at any time.

Soon, text messages became the primary means by which young people communicated, eclipsing voice calls by a wide margin. However, just like the farmer vs. Monsanto case, today's wireless technology has had its share of unintended consequences.

A decade or so ago, I would not have thought that teens would send naked pictures of themselves using text messages. Today, nationally, some surveys suggest about 15% - 30% of teens have used the technology for this purpose now known as sexting. *(NOTE: These stats depend on many issues and should not always be considered accurate as it relates to your child or their peer group.)*

Although bullying has existed since the days of the Neanderthals, did we understand that cell phones would be used in some cases to humiliate, bully, and intimidate other young people?

Did we understand that social media sites and apps would open the world up to our children, while also opening our kids up to the world?

Did we think about these issues before handing the phone or tablet over to our children without any education or boundaries?

As of writing this on September 2019, I have spoken to over 500,000 students and adults on issues related to technology. In the ten plus years we have been making these presentations, much has changed.

According to our 2019-2020 survey of teens and their use of smartphones, 38% of teens will admit to spending over three hours per day on smartphones and tablets. Another 13% admit to using social media for more than five hours per days. Some of them far, far longer.

The majority of this time is spent on a mobile device, sometimes outside the home but often in their bedrooms after midnight, losing precious sleep and creating eye strain into the bargain.

Our same survey shows that 32% use video games for more than three hours per day.

What does this mean for parents? Simply put, the way our youth culture communicates within the ADT is significantly different than even five to ten years ago. While much of this change is for good, it is incumbent upon us as parents and grandparents to understand and monitor the technologies our children and grandchildren are using.

How can you keep up with this constant evolution?

Well, this book is a start. We also suggest you visit our website, www.awiredfamily.org. Much of the content of this book is published on our site. Access this updated content periodically to understand the apps kids are using, the websites they're accessing, the new technologies they're using and the fads related to these technologies.

2.1 What is a Digital Tattoo?

So, what is your child's digital tattoo? It is the accumulation of data and metadata about your child's likes, dislikes, comments, pictures, current and historical location, and many other items related to what your child does on their digital devices. Most of us would probably have thought twice before providing these devices to our children, had we only known the endless information our kids would give up to marketing companies based on their use of free apps and bots—or by simply turning on their phones.

Allow me to provide an example from my parent presentations.

I often select a parent from the audience and ask them to pretend to be in their back yard, enjoying a cold drink on a Saturday afternoon. A well-dressed young man around thirty years old interrupts their respite. He says, "I'll give you $10,000 per month for a year if you give me the name of your child, their phone number, email address, social media names, their likes and dislikes and allow me to follow them seven days a week, twenty-four hours per day for as long as you provide that information. That's $120,000 per year. Will you provide that information to me?"

Regardless of how that might improve your chances for that lake house you always coveted, you'd say, "Heck no!" No caring and responsible parent would provide such information for any amount of money. These are our children. It's our responsibility to protect them now—and, as far as we can, from anything that might adversely impact them in the future.

The reality is that no smartly-dressed young man will enter your yard and offer to pay for such information. Why? Because if you allowed your child the luxury of a device and social media accounts, you already gave that information away for free. That, my friends, is your child's digital tattoo.

It's been reported that Facebook and Instagram possess ninety-eight data points on each of their users. Do we want that information in the hands of marketing companies?

On the other hand, Axiom, a large data aggregator has about 5000 data points on most Americans, ranging from your penchant for Starbucks coffee every Friday morning, to that ugly sweater you bought for your Christmas party.

Although many of us have a real tattoo on our skin, most, sans those acquired under the influence of adult beverages on Spring break, had given the ink great thought before going through the pain and cost of the buzzing needle. We select the designs. We decide where the images will be placed on our bodies.

We decide who the artist will be and what possible consequences there will be for getting such body art.

In today's world, unless you get a face tattoo, few professions would be unavailable to you. Regardless, that image on your back of a dolphin jumping a bottle of Corona Extra was your decision. Perhaps it was not well thought out, but it was yours alone.

With digital tattoos, your child did not decide to get one. They don't know where it is. They don't know who can see it. They don't know what the consequences will be for having it.

Our point? If your child is using an app, website, or digital device, they are creating a digital tattoo. If curated properly, that information can benefit your child. If your child does not properly curate their social media activity, it can create obstacles to their future success. This book will guide you through the ADT and immense evolution in communications so that your child's online activity doesn't hinder their future endeavors.

2.2 What is the Genesis of This Book?

Several years ago, when I came home from work, I sat on the couch with my wife Mary Beth, watching the local news. One of the stories involved a young lady who had just taken her own life. Although teen suicides at that time were not unheard of, the underlying reason for this death was unusual for 2009. The story caught my attention and my heart.

Months earlier, the young lady in the story had taken a naked photo and sent it to her boyfriend. Following their breakup, he sent that picture to others in the school. Before long, hundreds of people had this embarrassing photo.

The resulting harassment and bullying she received turned this once attractive and vivacious young lady into a shadow of her former self. Her depression grew until she could finally take it no more. She hung herself in her bedroom to escape the pain.

Having lost our grandson eight days following his birth, my wife and I relived the sting of loss through the eyes of the mother and father who had just lost their child to suicide. However, our grandson died of an unknown medical condition.

No one thought this joyous event would turn into a tragedy. Sadly, it was undetected and unavoidable. Conversely, this young lady ended her own life, a tragedy that as we know—after many years of researching the impact of technology on children—was entirely avoidable. Few knew how one click of her phone could play a role in the destruction of one human life.

The next day, I went to the management of the large IT consulting company where I was Director of Educational Leadership. I suggested we develop an education program for students and parents on the issues related to the misuse of technology. I received an immediate, "yes!"

Although this is where the story began, it has evolved over the years as technology and its use have changed. In 2009, when that young lady took her photo, she used a flip phone. Today, the overwhelming majority of students use smartphones.

The first iPhone launched in 2007. The Android didn't even exist until October of 2008.

In 2007, there were 552 apps available in the iTunes Store. By 2008, Apple opened up the store to third parties to develop apps. By 2009, there were over 500 million apps downloaded by users. Much has changed—and quickly.

According to Statistica, as of May 2019, Android users had access to 2.1 million apps. Apple's App Store came in second with almost 1.8 million available apps.

Global consumer spending on mobile gaming apps is predicted to reach 105.2 billion U.S. dollars in 2021.

According to Common Sense Media, if you consider the ownership of tablets and smartphones, total teen mobile access has climbed from 67% in 2012 up to 95% today. Consider it was practically zero in 2007.

Moreover, from my own experience in middle schools, the majority of 5th and 6th graders in Ohio, Indiana, and Kentucky have either smartphones or Wi-Fi-capable devices.

Sadly, the result from our 2019-2020 survey with 2500 thirteen-to-eighteen-year-old students in Ohio, Indiana, and Kentucky, shows that about 70% of parents do not have any idea what their child is doing on their phone after dark.

Additionally, most have no clue what apps and content their kids are accessing. Nor do most understand how the misuse of technology can impact their child and their child's friends.

I often say, "No one would give the keys of a car to their thirteen-year-old and say, *have a great night. Be back by 10:00 pm.*"

Sadly, parents often have no issue giving smartphones and tablets to their children with no boundaries or education whatsoever. Quite simply, many adults are intimidated by technology.

However, as we have discovered, a child can do as much damage to another human being with a smartphone as they can with a 2000-lbs automobile.

It is for this reason that groups such as Wait Until 8th were launched. The organization was founded by Texas mother Brooke Shannon. According to her bio, Brooke's goal for her crusade is:

"… all children should experience a childhood filled with outside play, long afternoons with books and puzzles and time without the presence of a screen. After many conversations with friends about the smartphone problem, she wanted to make a change in her community and hopefully beyond."

The organization suggests:

"The Wait Until 8th pledge empowers parents to rally together to delay giving children a smartphone until at least 8th grade. By banding together, this will decrease the pressure felt by kids and parents alike over the kids having a smartphone."

Another group called PAUS, which stands for Parents Against Underage Smartphones was launched for a similar purpose. Founded by Tim Farnum, a Denver-area anesthesiologist, PAUS is proposing a ban on sales of smartphones to be used by children younger than thirteen. Their website, http://www.pausamerica.com/ details many of the reason why such a ban should exist.

For example, this text greets visitors to their homepage:

> *"We truly are at an unprecedented crossroads in history. We all know that*
> *technology will continue to improve and play a huge part in our children's*
> *lives. What we are seeking is a balance, and we think as a nation, we have*
> *gone too far. There's no reason we can't stop for a moment and pause to*
> *consider what is best for our children."*

Based on my experience, I could not agree more with both groups. However, I have found that age often has little to do with who should have access to a smartphone. Instead, maturity plays a more critical part. It's hard to legislate maturity. If we did, many of us would lose our jobs—and a high percentage of government leaders would have never held office.

Above all, this book is written to help our society understand the significant mental health care crisis we have in our country. We can't blame smartphones, tablets, and social media for every ill in America. However, we can stop and ask whether unfettered access to social media and technology might contribute to the increase in depression, anxiety, and suicidal ideation of our youth.

The following graph highlights my concern.

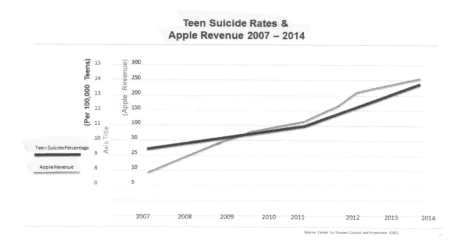

Notes on Graph:

The light-colored bar shows the revenue growth of Apple from 2007 through 2014. You see the company had unprecedented growth and at the time was the most valuable company in the world. Keep in mind, the iPhone was launched in late 2007 and significantly contributed to Apple's success.

The dark bar illustrates the year-over-year percentage growth of adolescent suicide from 2007 until 2014, roughly the same period. Google's Android Operating System was launched in 2008 and usurped the sales of iPhones significantly during that period, making smartphone technology practically ubiquitous among youth.

———

Is the growth of Apple revenue and teen suicide merely a coincidence? Maybe. However, it would be hard to convince me that social media is not part of the issue. At the same time, we have broken families, drug and alcohol abuse, a decline in family-oriented media, a drop in religious or spiritual faith, a post-911 generation that has never known our country not to be at war, the financial disaster of 2008, and a cacophony of 7x24 cables news coverage ripe with political discord.

All these have contributed to such systemic adolescent issues. Moreover, these have also helped to create the ADT.

Every children's hospital in the country is struggling with these same problems. Understanding the complicated relationship it might have with technology is paramount to the health of our children.

As parents, educators, grandparents, aunts, and uncles, it's incumbent on each of us to stop, look, listen, and analyze the problems and search for solutions.

When reviewing the ADT of teens, after the adoption of mobile technology and social media, we have seen many unintended consequences impacting society—but in particular, our youth.

We intend to help you navigate the landscape of teen technology use today and articulate what is coming down the pike in the months and years ahead.

THREE

Apps & Stats

E very generation creates its own standards for what is considered "cool." For example, teenage girls in the 1990s were often seen sporting Lip Smacker Lip Balm to school while wearing jelly shoes.

Boys might think all the girls would swoon over the scent of their Drakkar Noir.

Often, the grunge look took center stage in most high schools as bands like Nirvana, Soundgarden and Pearl Jam rose to fame. The halls of many public schools saw kids wearing dark-colored plaid flannel shirts, stonewashed or ripped jeans, high-top sneakers, Doc Martens, combat boots, and Birkenstocks.

Many, but not all, had "beepers."

Due to the many Rap music videos showcasing drug deals accomplished through pagers, the beepers of the 1990s had a bad reputation. So much so that James Fleming, Associate superintendent for Dade County Public Schools in Florida, once called them *"the most dominant symbol of the drug trade."*

Soon, schools that previously allowed students to carry beepers banned them due to the perception they could be used to arrange illegal drug sales.

In fact, they certainly could be used for such activity—just as easily as they could be used by parents to notify their child of a late pick up from school. The pager/beeper wasn't evil; what could be evil was only the person behind the small, blue screen. The same is true concerning today's smartphones.

Smartphones are not intrinsically evil. Smartphones are not responsible for the downfall of Western civilization. Smartphones won't lead your child to a life of crime and violence against the state. Smartphones will not cause anarchy within the Western world. These are all true statements.

However, parents often enable many of the very things they fear by not managing and monitoring what their kids are doing within their child's ADT.

Ask a group of parents, "What are the top three apps the kids at your child's school use?" and you undoubtedly will get Instagram, Snapchat, and maybe iMessage.

But reality suggests it will differ from school to school, geographic area, age, gender, neighborhood, etc.

In our survey, we asked about 2500 students between the ages of thirteen and eighteen (some as young as twelve and as old as nineteen as well) what apps they had on their phones. The results surprised us as well. Take a look.

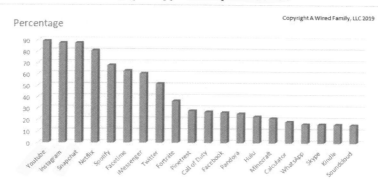

Top 20 Apps Used By Teens 13-18

What has changed over the years is the rise of YouTube by teens. So much of the music they listen to is by the streaming of music and music videos on this app.

You'll also notice the growth of Netflix.

While most parents don't think of streaming apps such as Netflix, Hulu, and YouTube Red as apps, they are a significant part of the ADT —and help to form sentiment toward the truth about their morality, politics, family, and more.

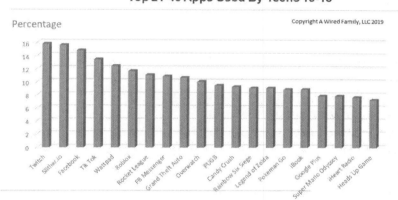

Top 21-40 Apps Used By Teens 13-18

Apps such as Twitch are generally unknown to most parents, but you can see Twitch growing in ranks among the top apps.

You'll see later that Twitch is a top app among boys aged thirteen to fourteen. Sadly, more parents *don't* know about this app than those who do.

Tik Tok is also increasing in the ranks.

Although it ranked 24 on the overall list – it ranks high among girls aged thirteen to fourteen.

Top 41-60 Apps Used By Teens 13-18

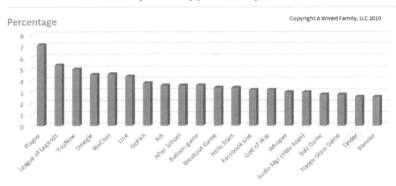

As we descend the results, we also find the use of apps that should concern parents. Remember, apps themselves aren't bad; it's what can be done with apps that presents a concern.

Of the apps I mention, please be aware of the dating app, Tinder. I discuss this app in greater depth later in the book.

Also, be mindful of live broadcast or video apps such as YouNow, Omegle, AfterSchool, and Facebook Live. Other dating or secret apps include Whisper and Bumble.

Top 61-67 Apps Used By Teens 13-18

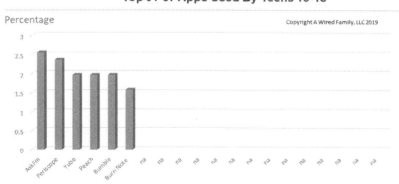

Differences in Ages

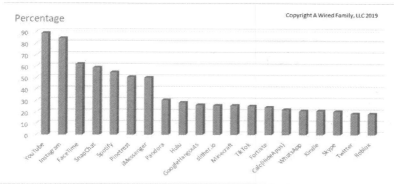

As one might expect, when you survey kids between the ages of thirteen and eighteen, you should expect some differences in their choices of apps. That is the case when comparing age groups and genders of students.

In the above case, we discovered that although YouTube was the number one app for all students aged thirteen to eighteen, it remained number one for girls ages thirteen to fourteen as well.

However, in some schools, Facetime was more popular than Snapchat, albeit that Snapchat always ranked high with young girls.

Tik Tok was the 24th ranked app overall for students ages thirteen to eighteen but ranked 13th for girls thirteen to fourteen.

Roblox ranked 20th with girls thirteen to fourteen and ranked a distant 26th overall.

Google Hangouts—which might be shuttered sometime in 2020—ranked 10th among girls thirteen to fourteen but barely registered overall.

There is an even more significant difference when surveying boys aged thirteen to fourteen and their use of apps.

For example, when surveying the top apps used by boys ages thirteen to fourteen, nine out of nineteen apps proved to be video games such as Fortnite, Call of Duty, Minecraft, PUGB and others, including Twitch.

We also asked students to tell us the top five apps they use the most, i.e., the apps they can't live without. The results might be surprising to some parents.

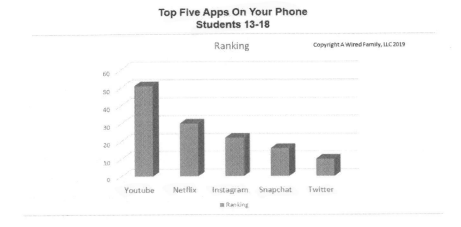

Boys aged thirteen to fourteen answered this question a bit differently, adding Fortnite to the number three ranking above Instagram. However, the rankings of YouTube and Netflix remained in line with the overall group.

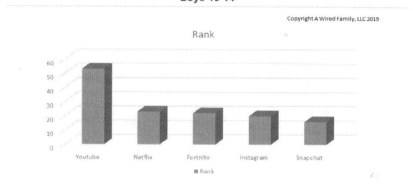

So, as you can see, the world of apps is quite deep and wide. Most kids are using their technology responsibly—but many are not. We will look at their activity on the following pages. However, our next chapter reviews how both children and adults have become so distracted by this technology.

FOUR

A Distracted Society

O ne of my all-time favorite TV shows, when I was a kid, was The Andy Griffith Show. In fact, years later while working in the video/film production business, our crew would often sit in our cafeteria watching reruns of the shows we had each seen hundreds of times before. We never tired of hearing the simple yet funny banter between Barney, Andy, and Otis. Life in the 1960s seemed so simple in an era of black and white images.

I recall the episode when a visiting preacher gave a Sunday sermon related to the fast-paced world of the early 1960s.

Dr. Breen: "What has become of the old-fashioned ways? The simple pleasures of the past? The joy and serenity of just sitting and listening?"

I suppose to parents in the 1960s, life *was* fast-paced. Rock & roll was on the radio, TV dinners were in the oven and Bonanza was now in glorious Technicolor... Well, assuming you had a color TV. Andy seldom had issues with Opie other than an occasional hidden turtle or frog in a shoebox in his bedroom.

How times have changed.

In real life, perhaps every child has kept something from their parents. A note from a friend, a diary, book or magazine? Kids are curious and impulsive by nature, their desire for privacy built into their DNA. However, as parents, it is our responsibility to manage that expectation and minimize the potential negative consequences of their online activity within their ADT.

The era of paper love notes and origami 'fortune teller' games that predicted who you would marry have faded into the ethers of the universe. They were replaced with YouTube, Netflix, Instagram, Snapchat, Kik, WhatsApp, WeChat, Yubo, Twitter, Tagged, Tik Tok, Whisper and a long line of social media platforms that cloud each parent's horizons. It's a time-consuming, arduous task to keep pace with our children while also bolstering our digital literacy.

While digital literacy should be at the top of your parental homework list, knowing *why* this is important is perhaps equally critical to successful parenting in a digital world.

To that end, we'll spend some time looking at the digital world as we know it today. Keep in mind that this world will be vastly different in five years. In ten years, the world will be starkly different.

I told the following story in our first book, Social Media: Your Child's Digital Tattoo. But it is worth repeating.

When I speak with students, I often tell them about a recent camping trip my wife and I took out West. We spent three weeks visiting Yellowstone and the Grand Tetons. Effectively, we planned to lock technology away and venture back to 1976, when we'd first visited these parks on our honeymoon.

What had changed in forty years? Well, for one, we were no longer camping in a tent. Rather, we were pulling a thirty-foot, air-conditioned camper. My long, brown beard and blond hair were replaced by a close-cropped, gray beard and very little hair. Lucky for me, my wife was the same as forty years earlier—although she might admit to coloring her light brown locks a bit.

During our first trip, we drove a four-speed, two-door StarFire Hatchback without air conditioning. We listened to an AM radio equipped with an FM converter. We also had our trusty 8-Track for playing music by Chicago, The Beatles, Stones, Jackson Brown, Carol King and James Taylor. Life was good.

This trip, however, we were driving a large, 4x4 SUV. We had our Sirius XM radio, DVD Entertainment System, OnStar, two iPhones, two iPads, air-conditioning as standard, two dogs and the aforementioned, thirty-foot condominium on wheels. If life was good in 1976, life was better now. Did we live without technology for those three weeks? We did not. But we came to realize how dependent we had become on technology.

In 1976, we traveled nearly 3000 miles navigating with a road atlas and an AAA Trip Tik. Forty years later, our map skills were considerably diminished by the availability of GPS and OnStar. However, to our credit, we did a great job of not checking email or doing Facebook updates. That was a modest success.

When we got to Yellowstone, it seemed almost nothing had changed. That was true for the mountains and streams.

It wasn't true for the visitors.

Standing on the precipice of one great waterfall, visitors seemed more concerned with taking selfies than enjoying the wonders of God's creation.

Were families really enjoying their dinners at the Lodge at the Grand Tetons, or was this the only place in the park where they had access to Wi-Fi? There were at least 100 people in a packed room, many with their noses buried in their phones or with earbuds firmly implanted, all isolating themselves from their families.

And while families still exhibited love for one another, there was no doubt that the earbuds and Snapchatting activity had driven a wedge between so many family members. However, this distraction does not just apply to children.

For example, each year, the popular Highlights Magazine surveys kids aged six to twelve on what it's like to be a kid today. They publish their results in State of the Kid.

In 2014, they focused attention on parental distractions. They discovered that 62% of survey respondents suggested that they felt their parents were sometimes distracted when they wanted to talk to them. The number one distraction? Technology.

This past year, I generally would ask my teen audiences about their parents' use of technology. In almost every case, at least 50% of the teens thought their parents were every bit as distracted by technology as they were themselves.

In other research published in 2014, Craig Palsson, a Yale economist, released his findings in a book entitled That Smarts!: Smartphones and Child Injuries.

In his abstract, Mr. Palsson writes:

From 2005 to 2012, injuries to children under five increased by 10%. Using the expansion of ATT's 3G network, I find that smartphone adoption has a causal impact on child injuries. This effect is strongest amongst children ages 0-5, but not children ages 6-10, and in activities where parental supervision matters. I put this forward as indirect evidence that this increase is due to parents being distracted while supervising children, and not due to increased participation in accident-prone activities.

As I mentioned, Palsson's study was conducted in 2012 when 3G was the dominant wireless connection. Today, 4G is ubiquitous as are smartphones in almost every household.

Phones are smarter, 4G is faster, and parents are growing more distracted as they balance work and family schedules on a singular device that is as convenient and flexible as a Swiss Army knife on a camping trip.

But on the horizon is 5G.

5G is *twenty* times faster than 4G LTE. 4G LTE's top speed is 1GB per second; 5G is able to achieve speeds of 20GB per second. Imagine how this will impact the content on your child's device. Imagine the distraction it will create for parents carrying similar technology.

According to CDC data, unintentional injuries to children under five rose 10% between 2007 and 2012, after falling in prior decades. One must wonder if the fact that Apple released the iPhone in 2007 is merely a coincidence.

In another report published in the February 2016 American Psychological Association magazine, Amy Novotney reviewed a study by North Shore—LIJ—Cohen Children's Medical Center.

In that report, researchers observed fifty caregivers and their charges at seven different New York playgrounds. The objective: to determine how often the caregivers were distracted by smartphones.

According to the report, caregivers were distracted approximately 74% of the recorded 371 two-minute playground episodes. Of those distractions, electronic devices accounted for 30% of parental diversions. These are distractions that would not have occurred ten years earlier.

Unlike parents in past generations who would often read the newspaper after dinner, smartphone technology is often interactive. It's immersive in ways that print on paper, or even the glow of a TV set can't emulate. Additionally, the TV or newspaper was never part of the Baby Boomers' or GenXs' job requirements. Today, many careers require employees to be tethered to the same device they use for their family schedules, entertainment, music, and work.

Then, of course, there is the deadly practice of texting and driving. While working at NCR in Dayton, Ohio in the 1980s, I would make the daily drive from our home on the west side of Cincinnati to my office in the Far Hills suburb of Dayton. The trip was exactly sixty-two miles each way. At least once a week, I would see a driver on I-75 reading a book or even a newspaper spread over the steering wheel during the daily commute. I recall mentioning each sighting to my wife because it seemed so unusual at the time.

In my work for A Wired Family, I drive about 33,000 miles per year visiting schools, hospitals and businesses as far north as Columbus, Ohio and as far south as Lexington, Kentucky.

I am on the expressway more often than I am in my office. By my unscientific estimation, one in five drivers of cars is looking at their phones while driving at seventy miles per hour. What was considered "unique distracted" driving in the 1980s has become all too commonplace in 2017.

Consider these statistics:

1. Distracted driving is responsible for approximately 25% of all motor vehicle crash fatalities.
2. Teens have been the largest age group that reported being distracted while driving.

3. Driver distraction is reported to be responsible for more than 58% of teen crashes.
4. In 2015, there was a total of 391,000 injuries due to distracted-driving-related accidents.
5. In 2015, distracted driving was considered a major reason for the 3,477 traffic deaths.
6. According to the Department of Motor Vehicles, nine people in the U.S. are killed each day as a result of a distracted driving.

Now consider that these stats are nearly five years old. Since smartphones are so much more ubiquitous today, the stats might only be worse. Regardless, these should be frightening statistics for any parents of a driving teen.

You're probably wondering, "What about that trip to Yellowstone and the Grand Tetons, and what did it have to do with distraction and technology?"

Well… I'm getting there. Perhaps the most eye-opening experience in our three-week camping trip was not the iconic beauty of the mountains, the tranquility of watching bald eagles soar above us while rafting the Snake River, or the frequent bear sightings near our camp. No, the biggest revelation to me was at a brief stop for a cup of coffee at McDonald's in Nebraska.

If you've ever made the trip through states such as Nebraska, you've no doubt experienced both boredom and fatigue. The long straight expanses of flatlands and cornfields tend to hypnotize you. Such was the case when we decided to stop for a cup of coffee at McDonald's which stood out like a mirage in Stephen King's Children of the Corn.

Mary Beth waited in the car while I ran in for the coffee. However, when I walked through the door of the restaurant, I saw very few workers. Rather, in the lobby of the McDonalds were large, digital kiosks that had replaced the humans that once took your order. What I witnessed in the middle of corn country in 2017 was the start of what is happening in 2019 and 2020 throughout our country—technology usurping jobs once done by humans.

Unless you work in the food service business, you might have missed how technology is disrupting that industry. We have been distracted by our own lives and thought McDonald's would continue to provide jobs for teens and retired folks. Inside ten years, most of those jobs will be reduced or vanish.

Two years following our trip, digital robots were being used by corporations for job interviews. In one case, the robots—powered by artificial intelligence—had interviewed over 10,000 applicants.

Moreover, the robots scanned the applicants' faces to determine if they were uncomfortable, fidgeting in their seats, or flat-out lying.

The facial scans could be forwarded to a facial recognition database. In turn, the scan could identify any online images or posts of that applicant in a matter of seconds. It's not fair, it's not ethical, but it's the direction of technology and society.

This is the yin and yang of the evolution of technology. It is good and bad. Technology is developed to make life easier, but in the process, often makes things different and more difficult.

The McDonald's kiosks will eventually eliminate minimum-wage jobs and they are already being used at other restaurants such as Panera Bread. But this technology will also open up new opportunities for such workers in other fields. It is a harbinger of what is to come and why education—and knowledge of technology—are so important to our children.

Similarly, smartphones snuck up on all of us. In 2007, with the announcement of the iPhone, who would have thought that 3rd graders would carry these into class each morning across America? Smartphones make life difficult for parents, but also allow parents who are willing to understand the technology to stay in communication with their children across thousands of miles and time zones. Times are changing at a faster pace today than ever before. The pace will not slow. It will only continue more rapidly. As parents, you must stay ahead of the curve.

That, my friend, is the digital landscape of today. It is the foundation of the Adolescent Tribal World State. Right, wrong or indifferent, it is the culture in which our children and grandchildren are being born. We likely all feel like Dr. Breen, wishing for a more relaxed culture. Technology is not going away—nor should it. It's incumbent on us to make certain we don't allow technology to run our families and relationships. It is there to make life easier, but we've allowed it to rule our lives and those of our children.

Don't be distracted. Be focused on the tsunami of change that is ahead, a change we didn't see coming that is examined in our next chapter on Sexting.

FIVE

The Sexting Generation

T wo years ago, I was asked to speak to a group of students in a small, rural community. The district was well-run and each year had some of the brightest and highest-performing students in their state.

The Superintendent explained that several of their high achievers had been trading naked pictures of their peers throughout the school. The county prosecutor was considering prosecuting many for the distribution and possession of child pornography. Those that had taken pictures of themselves would be charged with the creation of child pornography. My first thought was, "Well, there's not much I can do now. The damage has been done."

But I agreed to speak with about twenty of the offending students. When I arrived at the school, I was greeted by the Superintendent. He explained they had divided the twenty students by gender and assigned each group to a separate room.

He then asked me to speak with the girls first. When I entered the girls' room, I was somewhat taken back. I was expecting to see older girls, maybe slouched in their desks, bored and aggravated that they had to listen to some old guy preach about the dangers of sexting. Instead, I saw very young-looking girls, each looking somber and perhaps a bit anxious as to why I was there.Looking to ease their tension, I explained that I was merely there to help them. After a brief overview of my background, I asked if anyone wanted to tell me their story. Toward the back of the room I saw Annie (not her real name) raise her hand. Annie appeared to be a freshman, but later told me she was actually about to graduate.

I called on her and she said, "I would love to tell you my story so it might help other girls faced with the same decision that I made during freshman year."

She went on to explain she was now a senior, but during the fall of her freshman year, she started dating a boy she had known in the 7th and 8th grade. Up until that time, they had just been friends. However, that all changed when her friends started dating. Annie felt that if she were to continue to hang out with her friends, she too would need a boyfriend.

What started out as mere friendship transitioned into a romance during the first two weeks of September of her freshman year.The day before Halloween, she was in her bedroom reading, around 10:00 p.m. Annie heard her phone buzz, indicating a text message. It was her boyfriend. The text simply said, "hey, u up?" She replied that she was about to prepare for bed.

He responded with, "Send a pic."She knew that the often heard "send a pic" meant to send a naked image of herself. Most of her friends had received this message from their boyfriends. It was as if it was just another part of the dating ritual. Annie told me, "You know, kind of like holding hands might have been when you were a teen. But I told him no. He persisted and threatened to break up with me, and said if I loved him, I would send a picture."Ultimately, she gave in and walked across the hall to the bathroom where they had a full-length mirror. She removed her top and sent a topless photo. Annie immediately began to feel sick, knowing that what she'd done was wrong and might come back to haunt her. Many kids at the school already had naked pictures of other girls in the school that had been circulated.

Now, she might become yet another victim.

Weeks went by and nothing happened.

However, her feelings for the boy soured and by Christmas, they had broken up and the boy moved with his parents to Michigan upon his dad's corporate transfer.

By the January of her Freshman year, Annie was at the top of her class academically and had been a top performer on the girls' basketball team. The next few years were similar, capping off a senior year with a four-year scholarship for academics.

In April of that year, still weeks away from graduation, she was in her Physics class when a student messenger arrived with a slip of paper. He handed the document to her teacher who told her the Principal needed to see her immediately. Thinking that she had won another award, she happily descended the steps outside her classroom that led to the Principal's office.

When she entered his office, he looked upset and told her to sit down. After a few seconds of silence, he asked, "Do you know why you are here?" Annie responded nervously, "No." He then handed her a phone with a blank screen. He told her that he had not seen anything on the phone, nor had any member of his staff, but that the reason she was in his office was on that phone.

She pressed the button at the bottom of the device. A topless picture of her appeared. It was the one she had taken in late October of her freshman year. She sat silently and began to shake. The Principal told her that the image had been found on about twenty confiscated phones of students at the school.

She began to cry unconsolably and was walked by the Principal to the nurse's office. Annie remained there for about forty minutes when her counselor arrived to check on her. After a brief conversation, the counselor informed her that many of the students that had her picture —and those of other girls—were being prosecuted for the possession and distribution of child pornography. She suggested Annie must be prepared for similar action.

Within a few days, she was informed that indeed she was being prosecuted. Her parents hired an attorney and on her court date, she was accompanied by her parents, the Principal and a counselor.

Annie told me that that day in court, as everyone talked about a picture that took two seconds to click and send, no one was recalling her GPA, her academics, athletic awards or volunteer work. Every adult in that room was focusing on a picture taken by a fourteen-year-old girl who was still trying to find herself, four years earlier. She went on to say, "That was the worst day of my life, until one of the girls that had that picture sent it to the college that had awarded me the scholarship—and now, they've rescinded the offer."

At this point, I must fast forward and let you know that the university reconsidered their action and returned her scholarship, but it took the prompting of her Principal, counselor and coaches to change their minds.

But when I tell this story to students, I ask two questions:

1. "What happened to the guy?"

Answer: Because he was living out of state, the prosecutor didn't want the expense of prosecuting him.

2. "How did that photo return after 3.5 years?"

Answer: The boy had received a notification from Apple indicating that he was about to run out of storage on his iCloud account. He'd either have to delete files or move up to a more expensive tier of service. He decided to delete files. Year by year, he combed through hundreds of photos deciding which to keep.
After hours of viewing each image, he came upon the photo of Annie that she'd sent him during his freshman year. He thought it was funny and sent it as a text message attachment to his old friends in his hometown. One of the girls that disliked her then forwarded it on to the college.

This is an important issue that will create obstacles for many individuals of this generation. Almost 4 billion people have a cloud account that stores most of the images they take and receive.

For example, I have about 10,000 photos in my iCloud account. In fact, I've not looked at 90% of them. However, every photo anyone has ever sent me, or that I have taken with my iPhone, is stored in that account.

Imagine the embarrassing photos teens may have sent to one another. Some simply silly, others perhaps an attempt to appear romantic, while still others might be bordering on what would be called child pornography.

Now imagine this generation rising to prominence. Some will become doctors, lawyers, teachers, law enforcement officers and still others may be running for public office.

How many of these images will surface when opposing political parties—or others that simply dislike an individual—visit their cloud account in an attempt to ruin the reputation of another individual?

Warning!

These next examples are not meant to be political. They are simply illustrations of what inevitably will be a firestorm of mistakes made by this current generation that will haunt them as they rise to prominence in society.

Brent Kavanaugh

Let's first look at Supreme Court Justice Brent Kavanaugh. Although the Supreme Court appointments are 'supposed' to be non-political, let's face it, either party is not immune to attempting to find dirt on anyone they dislike!

Whether Brent Kavanaugh was a good guy, or a heathen devil worshiper, is irrelevant. Quite simply, it was incumbent on the Democratic Party to determine if the accusations hurled against Kavanaugh were true. In a "she-said/he said" case, they turned over every stone, and lacking a confession or recorded proof, they discovered photos of Brent Kavanaugh in his 1984 high school yearbook along with several written innuendos that suggested he was a heavy drinker and possibly a womanizer.

It took a lot of digging, but the photos and text written in his annual did cause him some embarrassment and almost a seat on the highest court in the land.

Ralph Northam

In an article published by the New York Times, Alan Blinder wrote about the February 2019 confession of Vermont Gov. Ralph Northam, admitting he was one of two men in a racist photograph published in a medical school yearbook about thirty-five years earlier.

If you're a medical doctor and the Governor of Virginia, one would assume your history had been well vetted by the time you graduated from med school and then ran for governor.

However, by simply again going back to black and white photographs from a yearbook, someone that didn't care for Governor Northam took the time, energy and resources to uncover a different side of a public, political figure.

In September of 2019, a similar situation also occurred with Canadian Prime Minister Justin Trudeau when pictures of him in both brown and black face surfaced in the media.

———

Today, no one will need to go to your child's high school or college yearbook to see them in their most vulnerable, immature, decadent moment. They will simply go to the cloud account of someone that knew them before they rose to prominence.

For example: Your son was a great football player in high school. He went on to college and had a good athletic career at XYZ University. He was in a fraternity, dated many beautiful women, graduated and went on to attain his MBA.

He married his college sweetheart and they have three beautiful children, each of whom thinks he's the greatest man in the world.

He worked for ten years at a major US Bank and now has decided to run for Congress. He is endorsed by his party and has been able to secure significant contributions to defeat his challenger that has been in Congress for twenty years.

The polls all are showing your son will defeat the incumbent.

The incumbent knows he's behind in the polls. His campaign

manager decides to take an offensive strategy I call "The Northam"—
i.e., uncover anything to cast your son in a dark light.

The campaign manager looks up everyone that played on your
son's high school and college teams. They look up old girlfriends,
particularly those that might be a bit down on their luck or felt jilted
by your son. They ask questions, trying to uncover any dirt on your
son from his past. Then they offer $1000 to anyone for compromising
emails, texts or photos.

Several photos of your son drinking at parties are sent to the
incumbent's campaign manager. An email is discovered of your son
using a racist term from his freshman year against another player in
which he was competing for a position. That player eventually became
best man at his wedding, and they have continued to be friends for
nearly two decades.

Your son's girlfriend during his sophomore year has a very
compromising photo of him when they both attended Spring break. It
is both embarrassing and potentially humiliating.

On Thursday evening, prior to Tuesday's election, most, but not all
of the photos and interviews with past girlfriends are released to local
news outlets and to national cable networks such as CNN, Fox News
and MSNBC.

Only having four days to respond, your son fights back, only to
have more photos, text messages and emails released to the public.

Your grandkids who love their father are crushed. This great dad,
husband and son has been unfairly attacked by those from his past.
His opponent cast him as a womanizer, a bully and a racist.

His election to congress is now looking unlikely. In the end, he loses
the election, his reputation and the admiration of his children.

All of this came to be due to human nature, greed and the cloud.

If you speak to your children about nothing else in this book, please
make this story clear. It will happen. It will happen with frequency. It
will happen to the best of men and women from this generation.

The genesis of this potential timebomb is due to what I call the
"Snapchat Fallacy" we will discuss in our next chapter.

SIX

The Snapchat Fallacy

I t was 2011 when I first heard of a new app that would allow individuals to send inappropriate messages without detection by others. The application, of course, was Snapchat, which was initially offered as a photo and video messaging application. To that end, users could take photos, record videos, add text and drawings, and send them to a pre-defined list of recipients. The Snapchat user could set a time limit for how long recipients could view their video or photos—up to ten seconds. Following that period, the images would be deleted from the recipient's device.

As with so many applications in Silicon Valley, Snapchat was developed to solve the unintended consequences of other applications. In this case, inappropriate or private photos and texts being saved or forwarded.

The genius of Snapchat had percolated in the minds of Evan Spiegel and Bobby Murphy. The application started as a project at Stanford University where Spiegel was a product design major. It was officially launched as a business in Spiegel's father's living room in September 2011.

What started out as a means of ephemeral communication and— let's be honest—safe sexting, had evolved well beyond the hope for privacy and was valued as much as $33 billion in 2018. However, by January 2019, its value had dropped to $8 billion. Competition in the digital sphere creates billionaires and paupers without bias or conscience.

Snapchat didn't start the trend of sexting, but it lifted it into the mainstream and made it feel safe.

But is sexting an issue among teens? The answer is, it depends on what you consider a problem.

Let's looks at the national stats.

According to Statistic Brain. 39% of teens between the ages of thirteen to nineteen have sent a sex message. Of these 39%, 37% were girls and 40% boys. The remaining 27% declined to answer this question.

A 2019 study entitled, "Singles in America" conducted by Match, the parent corporation of dating apps Tinder and OkCupid, discovered the following:

37% of adults aged twenty-three to thirty-eight said they'd sent someone a dirty picture of themselves.

25% of those in their forties and early fifties reported sexting.

Lastly, 11% of Baby Boomers say they've sent similar images. (Author's note: Really? Sixty- and seventy-year-old people sending naked pictures?)

If you're under the age of eighteen, this an issue at many levels, but most importantly, such actions are considered child pornography in most states when the sender and/or receiver is under the age of eighteen.

Then there is the act of actually posting such images on social media. In this case, 20% of teens between the ages of thirteen to nineteen have posted naked images on social media such as Instagram, Twitter, and Facebook.

But why do teens make such decisions? It varies – but as we know now, the prefrontal cortex is not fully developed until the mid-twenties. This region of the brain is responsible for planning complex cognitive behavior, personality expression, decision-making, and moderating social behavior.

Then there is that darn issue of raging teen hormones. Teen

hormones affect teenagers' moods and impulses as well as their bodies. Teen mood changes are caused by fluctuations in estrogen, progesterone, and testosterone—the sex hormones. These affect the way teens think about sex—or, should I say, the way they can't stop thinking about sex!

Let's also not forget that today's media culture is flooded with half-naked images of stars who flaunt their bodies as if they're selling sleek, expensive automobiles. You only need to look at the Victoria's Secret TV spots appearing during family television viewing and football games.

Society has given its tacit approval for such behavior. There's more on this in our next chapter.

Or, consider the TV shows such as Keeping up with the Kardashians, Big Brother and The Bachelor. Each of these programs sells sex as a commodity and something that should occur on a first date.

Lastly, did I mention raging hormones?

In our 2018-2019 student survey with teens in Ohio, Indiana, and Kentucky, we discovered the following:

- 25% of teens have sent sexual content to someone
- Over 60% of teens knew someone that had sent such information to a person.

In reality, many teen boys and girls today use sexting as a means to be—what they perceive to be—fun or flirtatious. Some suggest that while they may be "virtually having a sexual relationship" by using sexually suggestive words and images, that does not mean they are sexually active in real life.

Conversely, young adults suggest exchanging sexually suggestive content makes dating or hooking up with others more likely. This is often seen on college campuses. To that end, exchanging sexually suggestive content—especially as the teen transitions into a young adult—means there can be an expectation of real sex when they meet in person.

In an October 6th, 2014 article in the Washington Post, the

newspaper asked the question, "Is Sexting The New First Base?" The article was based on a 2012 study conducted by the Journal of Pediatrics. Below is an excerpt:

"The findings are from within the original 2012 study, done during a six year period. A diverse group of almost 1,000 adolescents in Southeast Texas answered anonymous surveys detailing their history of sexting (or sending sexually explicit images to another person electronically), sexual activity and other behaviors. It found that one in four teens had sexted and that sexting was, in fact, related to sexual behavior."

So, should parents be concerned?

Absolutely! Anyone, teen or adult, sending inappropriate material should be a matter for concern. Although I believe there are still many more good people in the world than bad, it only takes one person who does not have the best interest of you or your child at heart, to ruin a life. One misguided, inappropriate photo or video in the hands of the wrong person can alter the life of anyone.

That image is part of your child's digital tattoo. Once sent, your kid loses total control of that picture. Remember, the cloud might not be your child's friend in five, ten, twenty or thirty years.

Steve Franzen, Kentucky's Campbell County Attorney, has worked with me in his county for several years. Campbell County, although growing, is still rather rural. Whether we're talking about the inner-city of Los Angeles or a rural community in Kentucky, sexting should be a growing concern for parents.

In my 2018 survey among prosecutors, Steve said:

"Teens sharing naked photos is a common occurrence in our office, and our local police must contend with it. Unfortunately, sometimes—not always, but sometimes—we must bring criminal charges for these acts, such as the distribution of obscene material, use of a minor in a sexual performance, possession or viewing of matter portraying a sexual performance by a minor, possession of child pornography, etc. The penalty for violating these laws is extremely serious. Even adults who knowingly acquiesce in their teen's actions may be subjected to criminal liability for contributing to the delinquency of a

minor or facilitating in the production, distribution, or possession of child pornography.

"Unfortunately, more than once, we have had to bring charges against teens involved in videoing sex acts committed by their friends and "publishing" those acts via Snapchat, or some other social media app. All of the juveniles involved, those engaged in the sex act, those who recorded it on their cell phone and those who posted it on social media had to be prosecuted in juvenile court."

This, of course, is not a new thing, nor one with only local implications. Neither is it simply a legal issue. Consider Amanda Todd and the many other girls who provided inappropriate images of themselves thinking they would be kept private. Unfortunately for Amanda, it led to constant hostility, cyber-bullying and ultimately her suicide in October of 2012. The same was true for Jessica Logan whose naked photograph that had been sent to her boyfriend found its way to hundreds of other phones in her school and community after she broke up with him.

On July 3, 2008, Jessica returned from the funeral of a boy who had taken his life. Upon arriving home, she took her own. Her mom discovered her hanging in the closet with Jessica's cell phone on the floor nearby.

Other similar instances occurred with Audrie Pott, thirteen-year-old Hope Witsell, and many other young women.

After having spoken to nearly 500,000 people on the issues of social media, the stories I hear about sexting are seldom surprising. Most of the stories are often similar and involve the sequence of steps below:

1. Girl gets boyfriend
2. Boy eventually asks for naked photo
3. Girl says no
4. Boy says he'll break up if she doesn't send the photo
5. Girl sends photo
6. Girl finally breaks up with boy
7. Boy is mad and shares the photo

8. Girl gets shamed while the image is posted on social media and shared via texting apps
9. School discovers naked picture on phones throughout the school
10. Police are called to the school, law enforcement and parents decide the consequences.

About six years ago, I was presenting to a small, rural Catholic high school. During the question-and-answer period, a freshman girl raised her hand with a comment rather than a question.

I called on her and she said:

"Mr. Smith, you have no idea the pressure that boys put on us to send topless or naked photos. It's probably like the pressure you received in your generation to smoke. However, you knew if you smoked one cigarette, it wouldn't cause cancer. However, one photo could ruin our lives."

I remember thinking how mature it was of her to stand up and say this is front of the entire school. I also recall thinking, "If this is happening at a small, rural Catholic school, what is taking place in the large, urban public schools?"

However, the blame should not rest squarely on the shoulders of boys. We have discovered that girls are sometimes the aggressors, sending unsolicited images as a means of flirting or to attract a boyfriend. This is all part of the ADT.

In 2017 during a visit to a high school, a group of freshman boys was talking to me about social media. The issue of sending inappropriate images was mentioned by one of the young men.

I noticed that as we talked, he kept looking at his phone. Since it was an informal conversation with a group of his friends, I didn't think much about it. However, I asked him if the practice of sexting was an issue at his large suburban school.

Without hesitation, he nodded yes and then held up his phone. Sadly, a girl had just sent him a topless photo.

We've discussed national surveys but it's important to understand that we can't assume national surveys parallel local experiences.

Sexting will vary from city to city and school to school. In our study within a 100-mile radius of Cincinnati, Ohio we discovered that what happens in one school is often entirely different than a school just a few miles away. Teens are impacted by their peers often more than what they see and read on the web, TV and through apps.

However, sexting does happen in almost every school to some degree. It generally starts around the 6th grade. On more than one occasion, I've had schools contact me to speak with students that have sent such images. In one case, a bright, athletic young lady had sent a picture when she was a freshman to her then boyfriend. She broke up with him and never made a similar mistake again. But much like in my earlier example, it returned only to cause her heartbreak, embarrassment and humiliation.

In another case, a thirteen-year-old girl we'll call Megan was dating a fourteen-year-old boy at a high school two miles from her school. Like so many young men, he asked her for a photo. She said no. He suggested he'd break up with her if she didn't. She was in love and didn't want to lose him, so she gave in.

Sadly, he immediately posted the photo to Instagram. Within twenty minutes, twenty girls at the school heard about the picture on Instagram and downloaded the image to their own devices. Within thirty minutes of Megan sending the photo, she was being bullied and shamed by five of those girls via text messages.

6.1 The Worst Case Imaginable

In our first book, Steve Franzen provided one of the most disturbing sexting stories I'd ever heard when I inquired about such cases in his county. Here's the detail:

> "Detectives received a report from Missing and Exploited Children regarding a seven-year-old female who had been discovered on a Twitter account which was initiated by the seven-year-old. There were videos which showed the child in various stages of undress and exposure, encouraged by live viewers in Twitter and Periscope streams.

"The child was dancing proactively in her underwear, bra, and touching herself and pointing the camera directly at her private area. The video also showed that the child was taking care of her three younger siblings at home while her parents were out.

"One video lasted over forty minutes where she is taking care of the children with no adult present and while she is posting videos and interacting live with viewers who made comments about her posts. The online viewers seem to be enticing her to expose herself in these videos, and the child can be heard discussing the comments made by the viewers.

"In another video, the child victim appears to hold a child, change a diaper and talks about feeding the infant every day while mom is sleeping.

"A search warrant was obtained and executed for the devices. A dependency, abuse and neglect petition was filed, and all children were removed from the parents' custody."

Another case in Steve's jurisdiction involved sexting on a school bus.

"A juvenile, sixteen years of age, participated in using his phone to videotape a sexual act that was taking place on a school bus.

"After finishing the taping, he proceeded to place the video on social media, which was viewed by many individuals in a span of a few hours. The principal of the high school saw the video and immediately notified the police.

"The juveniles involved were picked up and received these charges:

1. *Distribution of Obscene Material to Minors – 1ˢᵗ Offense*
2. *Distribution of Obscene Matter One Unit of Material*
3. *Possess/View Matter Portray Sexual Performance by a Minor (1)*
4. *Promoting Sex Performance by Minor under 16 Years of Age (1)*

"The cases were reviewed by the Chief Assistant Attorney, and he made the decision to send the juveniles to Court for formal proceedings in relation to these charges. When the cases were heard in court before the Judge, it was decided to send all the juveniles involved to the Court Designated Worker's Office so they could be sentenced to Diversion."

Additionally, most of us think there is just one monolithic computer where Instagram, Facebook, and other services store your images, videos and words. However, quite the contrary. Instagram, Facebook, Twitter and other such services have hundreds of web servers where these images are stored. That's one reason why it often takes a while for your edits and deletions to show up on these services. Additionally, there are also web servers such as Akamai that cache your pages to speed up the download of your images to visitors of your social media pages.

I mentioned earlier the issue of having cloud accounts. This played a major role in the case of Megan. Each one of the students that downloaded her image to their devices had cloud accounts.

When they went home that evening from school and their phones sensed the Wi-Fi in the home, those images got backed up to the cloud. Those twenty naked photos became forty naked photos.

Given that so many colleges and employers now look at your child's social media accounts before they accept or hire applicants, having naked photos on web servers around the globe is an unforeseen consequence that this generation is just now facing.

Take, for example, this past Presidential campaign. You'll recall each candidate jockeying to find material from their opponent's youth that might damage their reputation. These were two 70-year-old people that grew up in an era without millions of cell phones and social media sites capable of capturing every embarrassing action of their youth.

I mentioned this in our last chapter, but it bears repeating: Today's generation will not have the luxury of their past actions hidden in the darkness of their memories.

Many of their misdeeds, actions, and lapses in judgment will be captured and waiting for this generation's rise to prominence in business, education or politics.

Imagine how high that bar might be in the future to secure the favor and judgment of the press, their country, and their own children.

6.2 Social Credit Score

Perhaps you have heard of China's Social Credit Score?

In that country, a number is provided to every citizen. The larger the number, the better you are perceived as a human being. For example, a three-digit number between 350 and 950 would determine whether you are approved for a loan or may travel outside of China. Additionally, since the public has access to your score, it can impact who might want to date you.

This system started in 2014 and can include how you behave on social media. Sexting, bullying, and boasting can all lower your score.

While such a system does not yet exist per se within the United States, it does in fact exist within some industries. For example: Life insurance and motor insurance companies may alter your premiums based on your social media posts.

In fact, if you're making a claim for damages in a personal injury suit or you make a large motor claim, a team of claims handlers and internal or external investigators will invariably look at your social media posts to see how limited you appear by your claimed injuries and to observe your daily activities.

Investigation tools and operatives may look at your online activities in many contexts—often illegally. However, in evidence-gathering, these things happen!

Additionally, PatronScan has a database of customers that should be excluded from bars and restaurants.

Airbnb has a similar database.

How long before the mistakes of our youth impact a future social credit score in our country?

6.3 Sexting & Parental Liability

In my earlier book, I mentioned that a few years earlier, Lawyers.com asked famed attorney Gloria Allred to provide some legal perspective on teen sexting. Below are just a few issues she broached:

- Teens participating in "sexting" activities—those that send and receive the sexually explicit photos—are at risk of potential criminal charges for child pornography or criminal use of a communication device, and in some states, face the exposure of having to register as a sex offender, a stigma that could haunt them the rest of their lives.
- If a parent knows his/her minor is engaging in "sexting" activities and does nothing to prevent it, that parent is at risk of being charged criminally with contributing to the delinquency of a minor.
- The parents of a "sexting" minor might have to pay monetary damages to the recipient if it is found that the parents were negligent in supervising their child and/or failed to adequately discipline their child after the discovery that their child was engaged in "sexting."

As you can see, parents seldom consider what their own liability might be should their child be involved in such actions.

Recently, I asked several prosecutors in Ohio and Kentucky to provide their opinion on how parents should handle sexting.

Dotty Smith, Chief Assistant Prosecutor, Municipal/Juvenile Divisions of the Clermont County Prosecutor's Office said the following:

"Parents need to talk to their children about their preference. It is important that the parent/child does not download the image or send it on as those actions are crimes. The preference is that those kids treat unsolicited pictures/message like their parents would treat junk mail. Throw it away/delete it.

"However, if the child/parent is concerned about the safety of the individual depicted in the image, the police should be notified. Again, the parent/child should not download or send the image. Place the electronic device into airplane mode and take it to the school resource officer or police station to report the concerns.

"Many parents/children are concerned they will be arrested. However, in our county, we prosecute the malicious act or illegal actions, we do not prosecute the innocent individuals who are simply bringing the crime to the attention to the authorities. Every action taken on an electronic device leaves an electronic footprint; the police will be able to determine who engaged in illegal or malicious behavior regarding that image and who simply received the junk mail."

Steve Franzen, Kentucky's Campbell County Attorney, said:

"We advise the recipients of such images to contact their local police authorities promptly. The police in Campbell County are all too familiar with this type of scenario and are more than capable of investigating and handling these activities.

"Not every instance will result in charges, but every instance will be investigated. Whether criminal charges will be brought is "fact specific" and made on a case-by-case basis, i.e., the age of the participants, their history with this type of behavior, frequency, etc."

Since many of our readers are not living in Ohio, Indiana, and Kentucky, I'd like to provide my own perspective on how parents should handle such situations should they arise.

However, before I continue, allow me to make a disclaimer. I am not an attorney, nor am I offering legal advice. You should always contact a legal authority in your state before pursuing such issues.

That said, I have had the great privilege of having talked to many prosecutors, police officers, school counselors, psychiatrists, psychologists, principals, parents, grandparents and children concerning this issue. To date, almost 500,000 people have heard our presentations. Many of them have told us their own stories.

Having lived in the media and technology business most of my adult life—and now having worked with so many schools on social media issues—I feel uniquely qualified to at least offer some advice.

With that disclaimer and background information in mind, I suggest you consider the following should your child receive a naked or sexual photo of someone under the age of eighteen:

- Talk with your child about the situation. Ask if they forwarded the photo to anyone. If they did, understand that they could be charged with distribution of child pornography. Discover as much as you can about the situation. As many people in the mental health and legal fields will tell you, this can have a tremendous psychological and legal impact on your child.
- Depending on the state and your school, there could be mandatory reporting requirements, which might require you to inform law enforcement. Although most states will work with you, others could make the situation more daunting for you and your child.
- In some counties, although not mandatory, it is suggested that you report the photo to your local police. However, you must also be realistic about the long and short-term consequences. For this reason, I suggest you consider speaking first with the other child's parents. However, if a naked or sexual photo depicting the genitals of a minor was sent or distributed with the intent to harm your child, I recommend talking with law enforcement immediately and perhaps seek legal counsel for your child. You know your child best. If you feel this will make issues worse, weigh your decision against your child's state of mind. This can have a tremendous impact on their school life and emotions.
- If your children have received any nude, or sexualised pictures depicting the exposed genitals of a minor on their phones, I

suggest they delete the image. Keep in mind, even when deleted, the image still exists on the device. However, you and your child do not want the potential legal consequences related to possession of child pornography. Make sure a copy of that image is NOT stored on another device or in one of your cloud accounts. Be aware, too, that the law in the US differs from state to state; just do not take any risks with this because what you 'think' may be acceptable in a state may land your child in deep water with law enforcement. Simply ensure your child deletes any sexualized images, and if in doubt whether the images can be construed as child pornography, get rid of them. Note also that the same kinds of stringent laws about possession of child pornography exist the world over—so just because I keep say 'in the US' don't think that it doesn't apply to you or your child living elsewhere.

- Given the rise in teen depression over the past ten years, I also suggest you seek help from a counselor or therapist for your child.

Regardless of whether the consequences are moral, legal or emotional, mistakes today will live forever. And forever is a very long time.

6.4 Sextortion & The Cobra Effect

During the era of British rule in India, the government was concerned about the growing cobra population. To eliminate the serpents, the government offered a bounty for every dead cobra brought to their offices. At first, the plan seemed to work. However, humans being human, an industry was born as stealth cobra breeding farms were launched to leverage the bounty for profit.

The government learned of the scam and eventually shut down the program. Those that had capitalized on the bounty were now stuck with hundreds if not thousands of venomous serpents. Rather than continue feeding them, they turned the snakes back into the wild. The result: India's cobra population actually increased.

In some ways, the technology that has developed to make some aspect of life easier or more efficient is similar. Today's apps have spawned their own Cobra Effect. Technology that allows you to take a photo and immediately send it to your friend can be used to humiliate others when posted to social media, and it goes viral.

The same technology that allows a soldier in Afghanistan to see his newborn child via Skype can be used by ne'er-do-wells to extort money or favors from unsuspecting, naïve teens, a practice known as sextortion.

We have heard a lot about credit scams whereby bank and retailer accounts are hacked and ID's stolen. However, those financial issues are eventually, albeit often painfully, restored. The issues surrounding scams such as Sextortion sometimes become permanent.

6.5 The 2019-2020 Sextortion Trend

Today, there are extortionists that trick their unsuspecting prey into performing sexual acts via apps such as Skype, FaceTime, Omegle and others—all the while, recording the acts without the knowledge of the victim. Once the recording is complete, the perpetrator informs the victim of the video or photos and demands ransom in the form of sexual favors or money. A study on this trend was recently published in a report by Trend Micro.

The trend exists in the United States and Canada with such cases as that of James Abrahams, who hacked into the webcam and hard drive of Miss Teen USA and many other women around the country—searching for inappropriate images—and then demanding more pictures or money.

In an August 2019 article in Moneywatch, a dating app user named Billy was the subject of an article on the current practice of sextortion.The female user on the other side of Billy's screen started sending Billy suggestive messages. She then convinced him to log onto Skype for a conversation that quickly became sexual. She convinced him to participate in live cyber-sex with her.

But as the article suggest, things quickly changed.

"Afterwards, the woman told him she had saved pictures of their brief cyber-sex session and was going to send them to everyone he knew... The woman demanded that Billy—who asked MarketWatch not publish his last name—pay her $800 immediately to keep the photos under wraps."

She then showed Billy the images she had of his actions and the contacts that would receive the videos.

That was only one example of sextortion.

Or, consider the high school dropout Tremaine Hutchinson who spent his unemployed days stalking young girls on Tagged.com. Once he earned their trust, he'd lure girls to send naked photos.

Once the pictures were sent, the extortion threats would begin. "Send me more photos or I'll send these images to everyone in your contact list."

Eventually, one of the girls was so disgusted by his threats to kill her and her parents that she told her father, who in turn called the police. Mr. Hutchinson was eventually apprehended and is now serving time in prison.

A 2017 study by the Cyber Civil Rights Initiative (CCRI), found that one in eight people "had someone threaten to post and/or post sexually explicit images of them without their consent."

The American Psychology Association published a 2019 study that discovered one in twelve respondents had experienced at least one instance of nonconsensual pornography victimization in their lifetime.

Although the threat continues here in the United States, it is of epic proportion in Asia. The Trend Micro Report details how the brains behind these attacks seduce their victims, who eventually pay significant fees to keep their videos and photos from going viral. One Asian group extorted $29,204 from just twenty-two victims before law enforcement caught up with them and uncovered a very sophisticated strategy to find potential prey, alongside the use of malware technology.

Although these scams have not yet grown to this epic proportion in the US and Canada, we must understand such threats do exist. With the growth of Facebook Live, Tik Tok Live, Periscope and YouNow, extortionists have yet another tool in their arsenal to lure unsuspecting teens and adults to do things they might otherwise not consider.

6.6 No, this is not new...

You might be forgiven for thinking these issues are just beginning to emerge in 2019 and 2020. This is not the case.

In 2012, Amanda Todd became one of the first widely known victims of sextortion. She was only fourteen and had unfettered access to her laptop in her bedroom. Amanda used several websites and platforms such as Facebook, YouTube, and web-camera chat sites. In time, she 'met' what she thought was a nice young man who showed interest in her. Sadly, like so many other victims, he groomed her over time and convinced her to send a topless photo.

Sadly, her life spun out of control as he threatened to send the image to her parents, teachers, and friends. She eventually succumbed to suicide after two years of threats by this man, in addition to physical abuse and cyberbullying by her peers.

Nearly nine years later, Dutch law enforcement arrested Aydin Coban, 35, for his alleged extortion of Amanda and many other teen girls and adult men, in Canada, the United States, Britain and the Netherlands. However, it's unknown how many other victims have gone unnoticed. Mr. Coban continues to claim his innocence.

6.7 Sexting & The Dark Web

In a USA TODAY interview, Amanda's mother, Carol Todd said:

"In the back of my mind, I never thought of a predator, I thought the person who wanted the pictures was an older teen. I never thought it was a 35-year-old man on the other end."

In reality, that's one of the greatest issues we face with our teens. We never really know who is at the other end of the communication. Moreover, it's difficult to gauge their intention or motivation. Amanda was looking for a friend and confidante, someone she could trust. Aydin Coban, on the other hand, was purportedly only looking for pleasure and self-gratification. Each chose a technology that was developed to make life easier, more efficient and pleasant.

Amanda is no longer on the face of the earth. Mr. Coban is in jail awaiting his trial. Neither was the consequence each was hoping for.

Had they both only known...things may have turned out different. Read more about the Dark Web later in this book.

6.8 Art Reflects Life

In the battle for content between Netflix, Hulu, and Amazon Prime, there has been a wealth of original and niche programming that would not exist if not for such streaming services and the public's insatiable appetite for content.

The Netflix original series Black Mirror unraveled the subject of sextortion with the production of "Shut Up and Dance."

In that episode, the program illustrated some unrealistic scenarios, yet the technology behind the subject is very much real. Moreover, as we detail in our social media presentation, 'Your Digital Tattoo', never before in history has it been so easy to talk, record and dupe our children into doing the unthinkable.

Does this mean our kids are bad people and we're horrible excuses for parents? No. But it does mean families need to be more aware of how technology can infiltrate our lives without our knowledge.

Just doing a simple Google search on the subject of "sextortion news," means you'll receive over 16,000 articles on the subject. Expand the search to "sextortion," and Google returns over 356,000 links on the subject. Yet, the issue and threat are generally swept under the carpet in our homes.

To explore this sad and sadistic form of online abuse, The University of New Hampshire Crimes Against Children Research Center partnered with non-profit THORN to study the impact of this abuse.

The study discovered that women were the primary targets, and more than 50% of these victims knew the offender before the harassment began. Moreover, almost all were under eighteen when the abuse started.

However, it also occurs with older teens and young adults as is detailed by ABC News regarding two George Mason University students that fell victim to sextortion after they were blackmailed with explicit videos.

Additionally, a Microsoft sponsored study shows that teen sextortion is escalating, with 44% of teen respondents suggesting they experienced sexual threats or knew of instances among family and friends.

One-third of those suggesting they experienced sextortion responded that these acts occurred nearly every time they went online. Due to the results of this study, Microsoft released some of the results early to warn parents of the online dangers.

Jacqueline Beauchere, Microsoft's Chief Online Safety Officer said:

"We've chosen to make this preliminary release, featuring data about teens in the back-to-school time frame to remind young people about the need for smart, safe and respectful online habits at home, at school and on the go. We will follow with an early look at key data from the adult respondents in the weeks ahead."

As we mention in each of our presentations, please understand that there should be no assumed privacy in the digital world. Almost every app has the ability to record the communication between all parties. However, generally, the majority of the times sextortion occurs is not a result of a hack or poor privacy settings on an individual app. Rather, sextortion usually occurs as a result of someone sharing a word, photo or video with a trusted friend or romantic partner. When the relationship ends, the offended party seeks revenge and provides the intimate results of that former romance to the world.

This happens to the best of people and their families—and it can happen to your family as well.

Please talk with your children and help them understand that in a world of digital devices, their words, photos, and videos can cause their young lives to spin out of control. Forewarned is forearmed.

A major component of sextortion revolves around bullying, the subject of our next chapter.

SEVEN

Bullying & Cyberbullying

I t is hard to read or watch the news today without seeing or hearing stories concerning the sexual misconduct of entertainers, politicians, news anchors and others.

However, often lost in the conversation about adult society is the issue of bullying and cyberbullying among teens and tweens. I can tell you from my work with schools, cyberbullying is still by far the greatest concern for school administrators.

In a July 29th, 2019 article in the Insurance Journal, writer Sally Ho tells a story about a young woman who had been cyberbullied. She wrote that the woman, "remembers feeling gutted in high school when a former friend would mock her online postings, threaten to unfollow or unfriend her on social media and post inside jokes about her to others online."

Does this sound like just the sort of thing we have come to expect from social media? Does it simply sound routine and, to some degree, acceptable? Does it make you feel the child should just have ignored it, blocked the offenders and moved on?

If so, think again.

Social media and online activity are now such a mainstream part of our teens' and tweens' lives that conflict here feels akin to having stones hurled at you each time you go out the front door. Social media life *is* real life, as far as teens and tweens are concerned. In fact, for some children, online social interaction may be the only positive social interaction they receive. So, kids feel that to be outcast here, means to be a failure. Their final avenue for approval has been cut off.

As in so many other cases, the events described by Insurance Journal's Sally Ho were so tortuous that the young girl had considered suicide. Following help from others, however, she began to limit her time on social media. The young woman, now 19 said, "It helps to take a break from it for perspective."

In an August 2019 broadcast and later posted on NBCDFW.com, reporter Bianca Castro ventured:

"Experts said a negative comment or a screenshot or video that goes viral can weigh just as heavy on a teen's emotional well-being as an adult who loses a job. They said it's because teens lack life experience."

Furthermore, in that same report, Children's Health psychiatrist and UT Southwestern Professor of Psychiatry Dr. Betsy Kennard said,

"Kids don't see the future like adults do, so when they're miserable they think they're going to always be miserable,"

There's a rise in cyberbullying nationwide, with three times as many girls reporting being harassed online or by text message than boys, according to the National Center for Education Statistics.

The U.S. Department of Education's research and data arm released a survey which shows an uptick in online abuse, though the overall number of students reporting being bullied stayed the same.

Two years ago, over 20 million people viewed the heart-breaking video of Keaton Jones as he told his story of being bullied in school. Like many of you, I questioned why his mom would post the video. But it touched the hearts of millions and brought to light the silent suffering of so many children due to bullying.

What has not changed in centuries is that kids have always tried to find out where they fit in. Teens by nature struggle with self-image and confidence which often displays itself in various forms.

Researcher, Dr. Andre Sourander suggests there are two types of bullies. The pure bully who has high self-esteem and no empathy toward his victim, and the bully-victim. The latter is a victim of bullying, who then inflicts bullying upon others.

Regardless of the type, both might suffer from psychiatric disorders and both are at increased risk for committing severe, violent offenses over time. Sadly, it often starts in middle schools.

If you are on the receiving end of the bully's fist, words or action, you likely don't care which type your tormenter is. Yet today, the taunts don't only emanate from the schoolyard or school bus; they invade the sacred, safe dwelling of most youth… their home.

More often than not, bullying today can take place online via text messages or social media platforms such as Instagram or Snapchat, or anonymous apps such as Kik, WhatsApp, AskFm Whisper, Sarahah and TBH.

Are kids' psyches more vulnerable today than in years past? Are they simply snowflakes that can't take the heat?

Not really. The difference today relates to the 7 x 24 access to technology. Bullies can hide behind the curtain of anonymity and denigrate those that they feel are weak. Since so many parents give unfettered access to devices, the bully can attack at all hours of the day and the victim receives and sees an unrelenting line of disturbing comments about their looks, differences, and sometimes outright lies about them. As we said earlier, 75% of parents allow their kids to sleep with their phones. This would seem to be fine.

However, kids are NOT sleeping. Rather, they are checking, responding, checking and responding to social media and text messages, sometimes all night long.

Will the bullies grow out of their approach to dealing with others? Likely not without intervention.In fact, in research conducted in Beijing that followed children in the 4-6th grades, they found that bully-victims didn't veer from the pattern of victimizing others over time.In an article penned by Internet Safety expert, Sue Scheff in the Huffington Post, Scheff reviewed a poll sponsored by AT&T and the

Tyler Clementi Foundation. The poll suggested that while nearly 50% of teens have experienced cyberbullying, their parents are largely unaware of what's happening under their own roof.

Moreover, only one in three children informed their parents about the bullying. As we have said for some time, there is a clear disconnect between teens and parents in terms of communication.

To shed light on these issues, AT&T produced the film, "There's a Soul Behind That Screen". This is an excellent, twenty-minute film for both parents, teens and tweens related to the misuse of technology among our youth and the possible real-life consequences.

Accompanying the film is a written guide produced by Common Sense Media and the Tyler Clementi Foundation, providing tools to identify signs of bullying and most importantly, helpful tips on to handle such issues.

But there are many, many additional resources for families, such as:

-AT&T's #LaterHaters resource page which helps you and your child block out the haters;

- The Tyler Clementi Foundation's The Upstander Pledge to unite communities;

- And the Cyber Civil Rights Initiative, a page for victims of non-consensual porn.

And while texting is often the source of pain for teens and adults, it can also be the source to help. The Crisis Text Line is available seven days per week, twenty-four hours per day to help your child in their most difficult hour. Simply text 741741 (USA) or 686868 (Canada), and 85258 (United Kingdom).

You or your child will be connected to someone that can help.

Also, consider accessing the following websites to download any number of family smartphone and social media contracts and pledges to keep everyone in the family committed to safe technology use as a family.

https://www.commonsensemedia.org/sites/default/files/uploads/research/familymediacontracts1.pdf
http://www.safekids.com/family-contract-for-smartphone-use/
http://www.connectsafely.org/contract/

https://www.teensafe.com/blog/creating-an-acceptable-smartphone-contract/

Additional resources in the UK, Canada and Australia are:

The Diana Award's Anti-Bullying Campaign (in the UK)

https://www.antibullyingpro.com

Bullying No Way (in Australia) https://bullyingnoway.gov.au/

Stop A Bully (in Canada) http://www.stopabully.ca/

And of course, please continue visiting www.awiredfamily.org for much more information about teens' use of technology.

EIGHT

The Dark Web

O ver the past year, I've heard several questions from students concerning the dark web. Three years ago, I doubt any teen or tween would have heard of this alternative network. However, today, it is the subject of TV programs, news articles and documentaries. Should you be concerned? I think so.

So, what is it? It might help to have an often-used example of an iceberg. (For those of you familiar with the dark web and have heard the example of the iceberg too many times, please forgive me and skip ahead.)

What most of us see would be the surface level of the iceberg. This includes search engines such as Google, Bing and Yahoo, and social media websites such as Facebook, Twitter... and news and entertainment sites such as ESPN, the Washington Post, New York Times and many other websites.

Most experts suggest that sites that are accessible through browsers such as Google, Edge, Explorer, Safari and Fire Fox represent only about 4-10% of the web.

Then there is 'the Deep Web'. Note at this stage, despite the name similarity, the deep web and the dark web are not the same!

The deep web is exactly as it sounds; it comprises the area of the iceberg that is close to the surface but cannot be seen. It isn't hiding itself for nefarious reasons, however.

This is the content of databases and other web services traditional search engines can't index. Some examples might be academic databases, government records and corporate intranets. These are not illicit sites, nor should they be a concern.

Then there is 'the dark web', something else entirely. It sits well below the surface and consumes perhaps the bulk of the web.

It's the encrypted part of the network where many illegal and, some might say, dangerous activities take place. Virtually every desire and illegal activity can be seen, bought and sold on the dark web, without leaving an obvious trial behind.

The most famous of sites on the dark web was Silk Road.

It's believed that hundreds of thousands of dollars of illegal commerce took place on Silk Road before it was shut down. It was perhaps best known for the selling of illegal drugs.

So how do you access the dark web?

The most common way to access the dark web is via the Onion Router, more commonly called (TOR) which 'protects' both users and website operators by encrypting all transactions.

It's easy to download and easy to use.

Other browsers that may be used – some of which leverage some of TOR's code include, Freenet, i2p and Tails. Still others that can be found in the iTunes or Google Play stores go by names such as Red Onion, Aloha Browser and a few others.

Keep in mind, not everything in the dark web is evil. In fact, much good might come from its use inside of oppressive regimes such as in Syria, Iran, China, and North Korea. In this case, the dark web affords such individuals the ability to communicate with other likeminded people without fear of being caught.

Conversely, guns can be purchased, child porn can be accessed, and hitmen can be hired, and terrorist activity can be planned without much hope of being detected.

In August 27th, 2019 the following story ran on ABC7 in Wheaton, Illinois. "A Des Plaines woman was sentenced to twelve years after she plead guilty to a foiled murder-for-hire plot. Tina Jones admitted she paid nearly $12,000 in Bitcoin on the "dark web" to hire a hitman to have the wife of a former boyfriend killed."

The company she attempted to hire was called Sicilian Hitmen International. She did all of this on her computer in her suburban Des Plaines, Illinois apartment.

In a March 28th, 2017 article in USA Today, Professor Aaron Brantley commented on terrorist use of the dark web:

'One of the things they do is...train each other on how to run all the traffic on their Android mobile phones through the dark web so all their internet and voice traffic is sent through encrypted channels and so unreadable by law enforcement.'

Ironically, what enabled the dark web was our own military. The TOR network was a government project developed by the US Naval Research Lab to protect government communication. I doubt they knew what would eventually become of such a secret means of communicating.

Now, should your children be able to access the dark web? I say no. Although there is a world of people in far-off countries looking for help, I suggest you leave that to the professionals that have the resources and time to communicate with those in need. The chances of your child seeing something or meeting someone that will change their lives for the worse is far too great to gamble.

There are countless stories of teens having been involved in illegal activities on the web, from buying bombs, to committing murders and posting them to the dark web, and human trafficking.

Keep in mind, this is an unregulated, encrypted dark world. Ethics are far and few between.

I suggest you talk to your child about the dark web and its advantages and disadvantages. Do this before they discover it through friends or on the street.

Help them to develop the critical thinking skills required in making good decisions.

Check their phones and computers for the browsers they're using. If they're using TOR, FreeNet, i2p or any of the others that we mentioned... talk to them about why they have the need for such encrypted technologies.

And of course, stay true to the steps you should take to keep your child safe that we mention in this book. This will help keep your child on the right path when using technology.

Although it's important to give our children some freedom, none of us would give the car keys to our child and give them carte blanche access to the darkest neighborhood in our cities.

The same is true for kids and teens on the dark web.

NINE

Parental Lack of Attention

I f you were stopped on the street by a reporter who asked, "what is the most important thing in your life," most of us would say *family*. Yet in practice, that might not always be the case.

We do love our families, but the demands of contemporary life sometimes force us to take the activity of forty-eight hours and compress it into twenty-four hours.

Something, sometime, has to give.

In May 2018, a second-grader shed some light on one of the biggest issues we have in America. Her teacher gave the assignment of writing about 'the one invention you wish never existed'.

The little girl went on to write, 'I'll tell you what invention I don't like, I would say that I don't like the phone.'

'I don't like the phone because my parents are on their phone every day."

She should not feel alone. There have been a few studies showing the damage parents can do when they are in front of their kids but are distracted by their smartphones.

Earlier in 2019, ABC's Diane Sawyer broadcast the TV News

Program titled Screentime. For six months, Sawyer and her team spoke to families, children, doctors and technology experts to gain their perspectives of this sea change in our culture.

Here are a few of her findings:

- Babies are impacted when parents turn their focus to a device rather than their child for only two minutes;

- American adults spend the equivalent of forty-nine days a year on their phones and tablets;
- The average teen gamer now spends almost twelve hours a week playing video games;
- Students do better when phones are not a distraction in the classroom;
- 70% of teens use social media multiple times a day;
- Tech companies design habit-forming apps to encourage users to stay on the screen.

In fact, a 2016 survey by Common Sense Media asked almost 1,800 parents of children aged eight to eighteen about their own screen time and electronic media use. Even I was blown away by the results.

On average, parents spent nine hours and twenty-two minutes daily on screens such as TV, PCs, smartphones, video games and tablets.

You might say, *but yeah, these are working parents.*

Perhaps… but on average, only an hour and thirty-nine minutes of that was work-related. Look, each generation of parents deals with new technologies that enter the home. My grandparents dealt with radio. My parents dealt with transistor radio and TV.

My generation dealt with Walkmans and cable TV channels like MTV, and eventually with flip phones when our kids turned sixteen.

But if you are raising a child today, you have the pressure of smartphones, tablets, Chrome Books, laptops, social media apps, reality tv shows, virtual reality and streaming media from YouTube, Hulu and Netflix, all of it available twenty-four hours per day, anywhere, anytime.

Moreover, this all caters to every niche interest, some good and some bad, including porn within nothing more than a click of mouse.

Your attention as a parent could not be more important than it is today. Additionally, social media and interactive streaming services and VR are immersive for everyone using them. They can rewire a young brain and play havoc with social development skills. Perhaps just as concerning, they can be incredible timewasters.

I was on WKRC TV recently. The young woman before me on set was a recent high school graduate who had already written three books. She, of course, was an excellent student, athlete and now writer.

She planned on going to college to study neuroscience. How much time did she waste on social media? Probably not much.

My point? We only have twenty-four hours per day. You only have your children for a short time. Of that, one third of their time will be spent sleeping. Another third will be spent at school. The last third, if you're lucky, will be spent with you. How will you use that time?

Cherish these moments with your children. They need you.

Recently, Jennifer Zumbiel, a young mom of four attended one of my parent presentations. Following the event, she told me of a game she was developing to help families learn to talk to one another again.

We got together a few months later and she shared the game with me. It was so well thought out and perfectly addressed the issues we have in American families; i.e., we just don't talk to one another anymore.

She went on to tell me how the game had come about. Her husband's client started taking each of his three children on a trip alone with just him, during the summer when they turned sixteen.

She says he did this because:

"We only have about twelve summers with our kids. The first two summers of their lives, you are just entertaining them, and by their third summer, the mutual memories really begin. Then by the time they are about fourteen, they are getting too busy with friends to hang out much with you."

Jennifer's game actually helps you jumpstart conversations with your kids that will really amaze you. That little mind that you think doesn't pay attention has some surprising memories and thoughts that extend well beyond a glowing screen.

Of course, I have no stock in Jennifer's company or any other product or service that I discuss on this program, but I think it's worth a look. You can find more information about the game at:

https://www.togathermoments.com/

I'm sure most agree that our kids are the most cherished things in our lives. To my wife and me, they are truly a gift from God, although I know at times that is not always obvious.

But how can we not talk with them? Even if you're correcting them, you are at least talking:

- If you are driving them to school, tell them to take their ear buds out and talk to you.
- If you are at home, put down your phones, lift up your head and talk with them.
- If they're playing a video game, perhaps you can play the game with them and talk about it?

Create time limits for any social media or video games for the entire family. The evolution of media that we discuss in our next chapter is impacting us and our children. The pace of change will not slow down. Rather, what's coming down the pike is both fascinating and troubling.

TEN

The Evolution of Media & Technology

E arlier in 2019, I undertook a quick study on how technology had impacted media. Not just what TV shows or movies were playing on Netflix, but a review of how technology had evolved since 1940, and what corresponding programs had been developed as a result of that technology.

What I discovered was both interesting and disconcerting. However, my concern is less about the programming content and more that the transition of what we might call G-rated programming to ratings of R or TMA happened so slowly, we barely noticed. It was as if our homes had carbon monoxide leaks and we were slowly lulled to unconsciousness.

In the image below, you see a quick review of the consumer "adopted" technologies available during specific twenty-years periods. By "adopted", we mean a large percentage of consumers were now generally using the devices. For example, the transistor had been around for many years, but the transistor radio really wasn't being used by a large percentage of consumers until the mid-1960s.

As indicated, the pace of consumer entertainment technology quickened with the passing of each twenty-year period. In fact, from

2000-2020, there have been so many additions, I only selected what I thought were the most used devices.

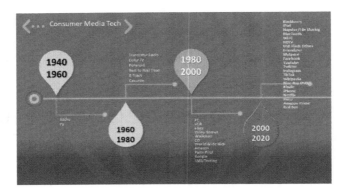

This image below illustrates the corresponding content enabled by the technology during that same period. I have labeled the general ratings of such programming during the decades as G, PG, PG13, TVMA and NC-17. I used movie rating since today's streaming provides a mixture of ratings for both TV and movies. Frankly, I needed to pick one.

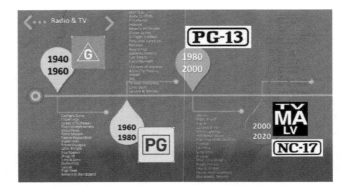

Is the technology responsible for the growth of more adult-oriented programming reaching inside our homes? Or are there other issues? The answer would be both of the above. However, the harbinger of things to come took place in December of 1953, with the introduction of Playboy Magazine. Up until that point, what we might call "adult content" was limited to peep shows and crumbling movie theaters.

Yes, there were the pornographic woodcuts in the 1880s, pinup girls in the 1940s, and Modern Man Magazine in 1952, but each stood outside of mainstream America. As TIME Magazine's Alex Altman wrote in December 2008, "Fifty-five years ago, sex went mainstream. Since debuting in December 1953 with a snapshot of Marilyn Monroe gracing its cover, Hugh Hefner's *Playboy* helped thaw America's once-frigid attitude toward human sexuality."

Indeed, once the domain of men in trenchcoats, Playboy became accepted by many American couples when daring men said, "Honestly, honey, I just like the articles."

I can still recall playing baseball in the street outside the home of a prominent attorney in our neighborhood. Having been raised Catholic and now in the 6th grade at Our Lady of Victory School, I was astounded when the son of the attorney told me his dad had a stash of Playboy magazines in his basement. "What? Playboy in your basement? But your dad is a lawyer!" Boy was I naïve.

Hugh Hefner became one of the biggest celebrities of the late 1950s and on through the 1980s. The once frowned-upon and risqué and airbrushed photos of woman in his magazines became acceptable, as long as it was kept out of the reach of children. But what really occurred in our culture after 1953 went well beyond color photographs between the cover of his magazine. Rather, the concept of sex outside of marriage became not only acceptable, but expected.

However, it all happened so slowly we barely noticed.

Playboy Magazine had gradually changed what was deemed acceptable on TV, radio, and in music, movies, publications and now even in the digital domain. The Golden Era of radio programs such as The Old Country Music Half Hour eventually gave way to the Ed Sullivan show which, for years, was the staple of Sunday evenings in living rooms throughout the fifties and sixties. Family sitcoms became popular, including Leave It to Beaver, Dick Van Dyke and Father Knows Best. Interestingly, the Dick Van Dyke Show network censors required Mary Tyler Moore and Dick Van Dyke to sleep in separate beds. But a decade after the launch of Playboy, the TV comedy Bewitched aired.

The characters Samantha and Darin threw caution to the wind and slept together in a queen-sized bed. Certainly, one might suggest this was a positive change, depicting a true married relationship.

However, with the growth of cable TV and the advent of MTV in the 1980s, music videos began to push the envelope, with groups such as Poison and White Snake creeping up to the line of softcore pornography.

By 1993, network TV was taking steps toward full nudity with the introduction of NYPD Blue. The show was often criticized for the state of undress of its actors, opening the door for other programs to follow in its naked footsteps. TV took on the responsibility of portraying the first lesbian sex scene on network TV on the show, Buffy The Vampire Slayer.

Although the show revealed the lesbian relationship between its lead characters early on, it wasn't until 2003 that they brought such a sex scene to network TV.

Perhaps the show that brought more sex to screen than any in the past was the one that actually used the word "sex" in its title, i.e., Sex and the City. From 1998 until 2004, the HBO series had multiple continuing storylines related to contemporary social issues such as sexuality, safe sex, promiscuity, and femininity, while exploring the difference between friendships and romantic relationships. Moreover, they spared no subject including anal sex, oral sex, masturbation, vibrators and the like.From 2004 until 2009, the Showtime TV series The L Word portrayed a group of lesbian friends just trying to figure out life. It also portrayed women-on-women sex scenes on a regular basis, albeit depicting both the physical and emotional components of such acts.Then there is another HBO series that took adult content to an extreme in the form of the series, Girls. The 'dramedy' attempted to illustrate what real sex looks like, including pain, clumsiness and embarrassment.

Why the concern with any of this content?

According to the October 2017 publication of the American Academy of Child & Adolescent Psychiatry:

"Every day, children arrive home from school to an empty house. Every week, parents make decisions to leave children home alone while they go to work, run errands, or for social engagements. It is estimated over 40% of children are left home at some time, though rarely overnight. In more extreme situations, some children spend so much time without their parents that these children are labeled 'latch key children,' referring to the house or apartment key strung visibly around their neck."

To the end, in the case of the early MTV programming, such content was available to any child whose parents had a base-level cable TV package.

In the case of the HBO and Showtime programming, the concern is that shows such as Sex and the City are available as reruns on the E Channel for most children whose parents have cable.

The L Word and Girls are also available on streaming services to which most teens have access on their phones or tablets.

Let me be clear, I am not a proponent of censorship. If you're an adult and you wish to watch programming depicting sex between two or more consenting adults, you should have that right. However, as adults, it is our responsibility to make certain children do not have unfettered access to such content unless an adult is present to explain the good, the bad, the correct, the incorrect, the moral or immoral components of the program based on your family's values.

Frankly, that is not happening in most homes.

Playboy's impact on movies was similar. Although there were certainly sexually graphic movies prior to the introduction of Playboy, such as Sophia Loren in her topless jaunts in the 1951 movie, Era lui, SI, Si, such movies were not released through major movie theaters. However, this began to change between 1953 and 1973. For example, the following movies are just a few of those produced during the twenty years following the December 1953 release of Playboy:

1954 – Two Nights with Cleopatra

1967 - Bedazzled

1972 – Pink Flamingos

1957 – Boy on a Dolphin

1969 – Bob & Ted & Carol & Alice

1972 – Last Tango in Paris

1965 – The Pleasure Girls

1971 – Carnal Knowledge

1972 – Le Sex Shop

1966 – Blow Up

1971 – The Last Picture Show

1972 – Deep Throat

1967 – Here We Go Round the Mulberry Bush

1972 – Fritz the Cat (Animation)

1972 – Behind the Green Door

Note: not all of the movies above were released at major theaters but did acquire a large following.

In an era when the majority of children have smartphones or tablets connected to wi-fi, and the top apps allow streaming, we are providing access to content not created for children. In doing so, we might be impacting the way children view sexuality.

Our next chapter addresses how such content—particularly that which is pornographic—can impact the young mind.

ELEVEN

Pornography

As you've probably guessed by now, I'm quite fond of reminiscing on simpler times, although from a distance the grass always looks greener. However, life was in some ways likely a challenge for our parents as well during the era of black and white.

That said, I can't imagine what it was like raising kids in the 1960s. There are many TV shows that paint a somewhat idyllic portrait of life during those times. Leave it to Beaver was one of my favorite programs. I recall one episode that depicted the rather simple problems Larry Mondello's parents had raising that chubby, not very bright classmate of the "Beave."

Script Excerpt from Leave it to Beaver:

Theodore "Beaver" Cleaver:
You wanna' mess around later?

Larry Mondello:
I can't, I'm grounded.

Theodore "Beaver" Cleaver:
How come?

Larry Mondello:
My father caught me eating pie in bed.

Ah… what parent wouldn't give a week's pay to have such issues today? Yet the 1960s heralded the start of an era that launched the famous Jacobellis v. Ohio obscenity case.

But what actually is obscenity?

"I know it when I see it" was famously written by United States Supreme Court Justice Potter Stewart in 1964 to describe his view of obscenity in that same case.

Stewart wrote:

"I shall not today attempt further to define the kinds of material I understand to be embraced within that shorthand description ["hard-core pornography"], and perhaps I could never succeed in intelligibly doing so. But I know it when I see it, and the motion picture involved in this case is not that."

I wonder—if he saw those images in brilliant colors and in 3D, would he have changed his mind? I wonder if he envisioned an era when every kind of pornography would immediately be available to every teen in 2019, 2020 and beyond?

The answer: of course not.

The images in question were tame compared to current standards. Today's TV commercials for Victoria's Secret might often be more revealing, or at least as seductive, to the thirteen-year-old boy whose evening TV show is interrupted by half-naked models selling… well, you know what they're selling.

It's difficult today for teens to navigate their own insecurities as their minds are fueled by raging hormones and their eyes and ears flooded by media's ideals of the perfect man or woman.

Sex sells everything from hamburgers, to cars, to beer… and we wonder why children are confused, restless, self-absorbed and often feel painfully inadequate.

Add to the equation the aforementioned 7×24 access to pornography via the web, and it's a recipe for rewired brains and a change in how this generation views intimacy.

The Origins of Pornography

Where did this all begin? Well, we discussed this briefly in an earlier chapter. But, frankly, pornography has been around since man first scratched crude illustrations on cave walls.

It was around 1440, thanks to our good friend the German inventor Johannes Gutenberg, that man discovered he could print multiple copies of the Bible—or, as others would discover, distribute pornography to the masses.

Then again in 1749, erotic graphic art was widely created and distributed in Paris, eventually coming to be known by many as "French postcards."

Although we think of pornographic films as a recent phenomenon, in the era of the roaring twenties, they were widely available to what we thought was a tame, puritanical society.

11.1 Enough is Enough

Perhaps thanks to the mainstreaming of pornography from the likes of the "silk-pajamaed" Hugh Hefner in December of 1953, viewers wanted more than the printed naked pictures in Playboy. Thus, by the 1960s, pornographic films were surging.

The growth continued with the development of video cassettes in the 1980s and with DVDs. In the 1990s, the pornography industry continued to grow. However, perhaps no one saw what was on the horizon with the Internet.

Beyond simply creating an immense marketplace for pornography, the Internet also encouraged many amateurs to post images of themselves. The use of webcams opened the industry even further, allowing individuals to post their activity live. Sadly, the Internet also increased the availability of child pornography.

By now you might be thinking, "What does this have to do with my child?" The answer: A lot.

11.2 Teen Pornography Consumption Statistics

What we think of today as "run-of-the-mill" pornography is being consumed by our children in unheard-of numbers. With Virtual Reality, it's about to get worse.

According to Therapy Associates, a Utah-based professional assessment and treatment service for children, teens, parents, and families, this is just a small part of what our kids are exposed to today:

- The average age a child is exposed to internet pornography is age eleven
- 93 % of boys and 62% of girls see internet pornography before the age of eighteen
- 70% of young men ages eighteen to twenty-four visit pornographic websites on at least a monthly basis
- 35% of boys have done this on at least ten occasions
- 83% of boys have seen group sex on the internet
- 56% of divorce cases involve a partner's obsessive interest in online porn
- 12% of websites on the internet are pornographic
- 25% of search engine requests each day are pornography related—approximately 70 million per day
- Only 3% of pornographic websites require age verification
- The most popular day of the week for viewing pornography is Sunday.

As teens and tweens become accustomed to porn, the next images need to be even more sensational in order to keep their interest and increase the level of dopamine to satisfy their cravings. This often impacts a user's ability to sustain relationships with their girlfriends and boyfriends, wives and spouses. Each new experience requires an even greater, more daring visual image.

Thus enters the world of virtual reality and the images it offers. But first let's address the devices before the vices:

11.3 Devices & Vices

There are many developers of new virtual reality devices and content. Oculus, Samsung, HTC, Google, and Sony are but a few. However, just to better define the interest as it relates to porn, consider the terms, "virtual reality porn" and "virtual reality sex" are two of the top ten keywords for searches related to virtual reality.

In an August 2019 article in The Sun, Harry Pettit wrote a lengthy article about virtual reality for posterity's sake. Couples can capture a virtual reality video of their "romantic encounters" to look back on when they're older.

A British porn company is charging £12,000 (nearly $15,000) to record a couple in VR, allowing them to relive the act in their elder years through a set of VR goggles.

In Japan during the spring of 2016, a virtual reality pornography festival was forced to close due to overcrowding. The venue was too small to accommodate the crowd.

Further, as Newsweek Tech writer, Seung Lee wrote in his June, 16th 2016 article following his first encounter with VR Porn:

"The moment I knew that virtual reality porn worked was when the naked, voluptuous woman began an oil massage as I rested in an armchair in a tropical vacation house in Hawaii. The massage escalated to sex in a hurry."

As parents, we must be aware a child's brain—in the best of homes—is not completely wired until well after their teen years. However, exposure to pornography can rewire an already underdeveloped brain before its time.

This overstimulation of the reward circuitry through *dopamine spikes* resulting from viewing pornography creates desensitization. When dopamine receptors drop after too much stimulation, the brain will not respond as it had in the past. As such, there is less reward from the pleasure.

Now, back to our chubby friend Larry Modello in the 1960s. Perhaps eating one Moon Pie satisfied his appetite. But after a while, he'd need two and then three... you get the picture.

This leads users to search even harder for feelings of satisfaction such as for longer porn sessions, with more frequency, and today through the ultimate porn experience—virtual reality.

A question for all of us: Once virtual reality becomes as popular as Internet porn, what will happen to intimacy between couples? What happens to families? What then happens to society?

Now consider that often, the gateway to porn is through YouTube.

11.4 YouTube & Porn

The overwhelming majority of teens use YouTube. In fact, in our recent survey of middle and high school students, YouTube was the number one app on their phones. However, type "virtual reality porn" in the YouTube search bar, and you'll be deluged with search returns with titles such as:

- Wife catches her husband watching virtual reality porn
- Trying virtual reality porn with my date
- Virtual reality porn is here, and it's scary realistic!
- Virtual reality porn with Nikki.

If you're not filtering YouTube on your child's device, your child already has access to the images and information related to accessing true, 3D virtual reality. Since fewer than 50% of parents monitor what their children do on their devices, this has become a significant issue for families.

11.5 Teen Viewing & Creation of Porn

My faith might very well be different than that of you and your family. However, I can't help but think of social media, search engines and our ability to connect all worldly knowledge—good and bad—to anyone and anything, as being something like the Garden of Eden.

The three major religions, Christianity, Judaism and Islam believe in the Garden of Eden. Whether the story is an allegory, history or simply a means of pacifying an ancient people, the relationship between man, knowledge and technology and that of the tree of knowledge is not lost on me.

Look at today's world. Think back to everything we've discussed in this book thus far. Are there similarities? Or is it just me? Has technology and its ability to provide immediate information on anything at anytime become somewhat a new religion? Are we now mostly bowing before the God of Facebook, feeling our isolated lives torn asunder when our posts are not 'liked', or when a neighbor happens to post a better shot of their supper, their dog or their new bedlinen than we did?

Is this what we have come to?

In fact, today's fastest growing religion might very well be the worship of technology. Keep in mind, I have made my entire career due to technology. This is not a manifesto against technology. But it is a grave concern to me as a husband, father, grandfather, uncle, brother and friend.

Think I'm exaggerating? I'll let you decide.

To that end, I want to share with you the results of a survey we recently did with teen girls. For example, we asked 2500 teens how many hours they used their smartphones. More than 70% said that they used their devices more than 4-5 hours per day.

25% admitted to sending nude pictures of themselves to others, i.e., created pornography on their phones.

Almost 70% said they had been asked by boys to send naked photos.

60% admitted that boys sent naked photos of themselves unsolicited to the girls, i.e., they distributed and viewed child pornography via their devices.

In a far smaller survey, we discovered nearly 70% of teen girls thought that viewing porn was either very or somewhat prevalent among their peer group. The percentage for boys aged seventeen to eighteen was well over 80%.

And over 70% of girls aged seventeen to eighteen felt the media in general media has put pressure on them to look, act and talk a certain way.

This might explain in part why 70% said they often feel bad or sad due to the use of their social media to compare their lives or bodies to those of others.

Through over-the-air media, social media and pornography, we have conditioned teen girls to strive for the perfect bodies, perfect lips, perfect butts, perfect breasts. These are sometimes obsessions with teen girls. We have also conditioned teen boys that this perfection should be expected.

How can a girl compete when today's companies are digitally scanning the bodies of porn stars for video-gaming sex and sex robots? This technology is here. It's not the future… it's here today.

If not properly managed, your kids today have access to porn and the creation of porn through sexting via apps on their devices.

A sampling of such apps includes Instagram, Reddit, Tik Tok, Tumblr, Yubo, Snapchat, and YouTube. Does this mean these apps are going to cause your kids to become heathen devil worshipers? Of course not. But they can change your child's perspective on true intimacy.

Although not always porn, apps such as Yubo and Snapchat are teens portraying themselves with sexual desires and availability. I see these children as crying out for help, love and companionship. They're not getting it from home, so they turn to apps and networks.

As Dr. Alexandria Katharkis wrote in her article in Psychology Today:

"When an adolescent boy compulsively views pornography, his brain chemistry can become shaped around the attitudes and situations that he is watching. Sadly, pornography paints an unrealistic picture of sexuality and relationships that can create an expectation for real-life experiences that will never be fulfilled."

This is not just a teen problem. It's huge issue in marriages today.

In a July 2017 article by Monica Gabriel Marshall in Verily, she cites a study by the American Academy of Matrimonial Lawyers who questioned 350 divorce attorneys and found that roughly 60% reported internet porn played a significant role in the divorces; excessive interest in online porn contributed to more than half of such cases.

With the increased use of porn among our children, one must wonder, will there be marriages in the future?

Pornography is a fact of teen life today. No longer is it an age of innocence. Even if your child doesn't have a device, they likely ride the school bus, sit in the cafeteria with friends or hang out in homes where their friends have such access.

Whether you use the analogy of the Garden of Eden or Pandora's box, I think we all get the point.

Who is responsible for this? We are.

We allowed this technology to enter society without proper controls. It's not the technology… it's us.

These devices are great babysitters. But what are they doing to our babies?

Now I've spent a great deal of time talking about apps and how kids use them, but there is one app that concerns me more than most. Tik Tok. We discuss that app in our next chapter.

A few final thoughts…

Because research suggests most pornography and sexual addictions begin during adolescence, Therapy Associates based in Utah provide a very informative paper titled: Navigating Pornography Addiction a Guide for Parents

Additionally, I highly recommend parents view the documentary produced by Channel 4 in the UK entitled: Channel 4 Pornography and the brain.

As the Channel 4 program illustrates, with teens, the patterns of brain activity when viewing porn are very similar to those of individuals with drug and alcohol addictions when they view pictures of alcohol and drugs. It is clear it can create problems for some adolescents and young adults who use it.

Moreover, as mentioned earlier, it's not just the addiction that is the problem; it's how these young people will view intimacy and relationships as they get older.

So, where do you go from here? I suggest you read our last chapter which will help you better manage your child's online activity and minimize problems for them in the future.

Virtual Pornography, which we described in some detail, is already a possibility on mobile devices and can already be integrated with your child's phone and certain VR gaming system headsets; it is, after all, nothing more than another app. (Augmented Reality Porn is available in the Google Play Store for Android users).

As such, it will be part of every parent's responsibility to manage their child's activity.

Parenting today in many ways is much harder than in the days of Leave it to Beaver. The temptations and access to pornography are greater at a time when both parents are working and have less time to parent. Getting your arms around the technology and temptations must start today.

Although technology is responsible for so much good in the lives of our children, I'm sure most of us would love a day when the biggest parenting issue we face is our children eating a moon pie in bed.

TWELVE

The Case against Tik Tok

F or the past ten years, I've been examining most of the apps teens are using. I've seen the evolution of MySpace and its purchase in 2005 by NewsCorp for $580 million dollars.

Conversely, I saw MySpace overtaken by Facebook in the number of unique U.S. visitors in May 2009. The sad legacy of MySpace continued when Mr. *Bring Sexy Back*, aka Justin Timberlake and Specific Media Group purchased the remainder of the site for $35 million and then sold it in 2016, to Time Inc. which was subsequently sold in 2018 to the Meredith Corporation.

To add insult to injury, CNN reported that the site, which was already on life support, had lost twelve years of music uploaded by users. You had a good run, MySpace, but it's time to hang up your hat next to DiscMan, Palm Pilot and Nintendo 64.

But as I always told our kids during their teen years, "things change." Everything of course except their dad's penchant for highly starched white shirts and Panera coffee.

The apps and technologies of the past are often lost in the fog of simply living life. Needs change. People change and technology perhaps changes the fastest. This is perhaps best illustrated with Moore's Law, which is the 1965 observation by Gordon Moore that the number of transistors in a dense integrated circuit doubles about every year.

Pretty boring stuff. You're probably sorry you asked.

Although most of us could give a hoot about the number of transistors in a dense integrated circuit, it helps to explain why most of us can't keep up with the technology our kids and grandkids use. Although teens don't know much about integrated circuits, it is the power of these technologies that enables the apps and video games they use. With each advancement of the underlying technology, the more they are able to do.

Take for example Tik Tok, formerly, Musical.ly. This app launched in 2014 as a benign little distraction that allowed mostly teen and tween girls to post fifteen second videos of themselves lip syncing to sweet Taylor Swift tunes with such urbane lyrics as, *"Look what you made me do, Look what you made me do, look what you made me do."*

However, much like society, the available songs from which the girls could select, morphed into other genres, more specifically hip hop. By 2017, the top songs were selected from the likes of Nicki Minaj, Drake, Jay-Z and of course, everyone's favorite and cannabis aficionado, Snoop Dog. So instead of Swift's lyrics, *"Is it cool that I said all that? Is it chill that you're in my head?"* girls might serenade their followers with lyrics such as "I shitted on 'em" or "I pissed on 'em."

Ah, few can turn a phrase like Ms. Minaj...

Considering that many of these kids were thirteen or fourteen, or frankly eleven or twelve, you can see parents' concerns were warranted.

By 2016, Musical.ly had over 90 million registered users, about nine times more than they'd had in 2015. By mid-2017, they reached over 200 million users. Today, Tik Tok is considered one of the fastest growing apps of all time.

Since Musical.ly had few if any parental controls, it became easy for strangers to reach children and children to reach strangers. As Marilyn Evans wrote in her article on the Protect Young Minds site, an eight-year-old girl was solicited by a pedophile within forty-eight hours of the mom creating an account with her daughter.

Evans wrote:

"Within forty-eight hours, a series of 4 notifications popped up in her account from 'The Real Justin Bieber'."

- First message: *"Who wants to win a 5-minute video call with me [Bieber]?"*
- Second message: *"All you need to do is send me a photo of you naked, or of your vagina."*
- Third message: *"Lots of girls send me these pics all the time and I will never tell anyone you sent one."*
- Final message: *"Message me now!"*

By the end of 2016, this once cute and creative app had dissolved into a cesspool of cretins looking to take advantage of unsuspecting kids. As one law enforcement officer told me, "For pedophiles, it's like shooting fish in a barrel."

Then came Bytedance, a Chinese company that owned an app called Tik Tok, who, in an effort to increase their user growth, purchased Musical.ly. They officially merged under the Tik Tok name in August of 2018.

ByteDance has had incredible success and is now worth $75 billion. In terms of stock value, it is considered by some to be the most valued startup in the world. According to App Annie this week, Tik Tok was the 4th most downloaded app in the Apple and Google Play stores.

So, Everything Is Better Now. Right?

Yes, and no. Parents had complained that Musical.ly lacked parental controls. Tik tok listened and now provides controls such as:

- 'Privacy & Safety' settings related to location sharing, private accounts, who can comment, etc.
- 'Digital Well Being' for screen time management & a 'Restricted Mode' with password protection.

While these are great enhancements, parents often don't take the time to talk with their kids and then add the controls by using a password their kids won't discover.

Case in point: I was speaking in another city a while back. To test the audience, I simply mentioned the name, Tik Tok.

Over 600 middle school kids erupted with either yays or boos. Keep in mind I said middle school kids of whom only a third were legally allowed to even have an account due to the Coppa Act. Don't know what the Coppa Act is?

That said, following my presentation on the overall subject of social media, many kids came up to talk with me and tell me their stories. A few mentioned that social media was in some way a reason for their depression, while others told me about their sibling's misuse of technology. However, waiting for me by the exit door were three girls. They asked why I was so negative about Tik Tok?

I said, "Because much of the content is not appropriate for teens." They agreed, but suggested it was nonetheless fun to see what other kids were doing.

Not to my surprise, the girls who ranged in age from eleven to thirteen said they were tired of adult men sending pictures of their private parts and requesting that they do the same.

Although they mentioned Tik Tok specifically, they later mentioned that the same had been true with Instagram. The question we should be asking is, "where the heck are all their parents?"

Having reviewed social media apps for so long, nothing generally surprises me. The downfall of AOL, Prodigy and MySpace will eventually befall Facebook, Instagram, Snapchat and now Tik Tok.

But why do I think Tik Tok might remain an issue?

If we look at the long tail of online communication in the United States, all have been home grown in this country. And while we often complain about the private information that the likes of Mark Zuckerberg consume from that device in our hands, we at least think the information he shares won't go to a foreign competitor/adversary such as Russia and China. (Overlook that little hiccup concerning Cambridge Analytica).

While the Cambridge Analytica kerfuffle shone a light on what information social media companies have on us, it perhaps did a better job of showcasing the issue of social engineering, i.e., "the use of centralized planning in an attempt to manage social change and regulate the future development and behavior of a society."

It perhaps is bad enough for a British company to illegally acquire psychographic information on 50 million users to aid an American presidential campaign, but to provide the private information of our children to a company with direct connections, if not full ownership by the Chinese government, might be a lurking catastrophe for our country—or any country.

Through the artificial intelligence (AI) that makes Tik Tok work, the views of Tik Tok management, or in fact the wishes of the "more than patient" Chinese government can attempt to change the views and even morals of a generation of Americans.

Consider for the moment the rapid technological change of the last century and how propaganda correspondingly underwent a massive change. Consider Radio Free Europe which attempted to change the hearts and minds of the Eastern European, Middle Eastern and Asian people. Consider the radio that Lenin called "a newspaper without paper… and without boundaries."

It was much easier to send a radio signal than an army to convince the opposition to your ways.

The difference with the above examples is that those messages were meant for adults. Moreover, the radio didn't have psychographic information about every listener. Additionally, the users of radios were not producing their own content that could be accessed by the entire world.

Images of your child dancing provocatively to Svrite, could ultimately end up in someone's cloud account only to be accessed years later when your child is applying for college, a job or running for political office. (By the way, the Svrite song and lyrics are NOT for the faint of heart. However, in July 2019, there were hundreds of girls on Tik Tok lip syncing to the words.)

But this is the world we're in. As adults, as a society whose adversaries have access to the most vulnerable among us, i.e., our kids, we must understand the use of technology and its potential consequences better than those creating the technology for our children.

Tik Tok has already been fined nearly $6 million for the collection of the private information of children under the age of thirteen. Whether they are an extension of the Chinese government or not, understand that all free apps tell us they are collecting our private information and selling it. This information is embedded in the Terms of Use Agreement all apps provide.

In the case of Tik Tok, that is why their parent company is worth $75 billion dollars. Demographic and psychographic information is the currency of this era.

Most of you reading this article were weaned on CD-ROMs and pagers. Some of you were thrilled when you first connected something called a modem to AOL and heard the shrill, almost alien sound of the device attempting to connect to a server far, far away.

Then there was the sound of *You've Got Mail!* for the first time and the thrill of sending messages through AIM, Yahoo IM or iChat.

This is a far different world from when you were listening to Third Eye Blind or Jimmy Eat World. Your kids are growing up with access to the world, and the world having access to your kids.

Things change. Including how countries wage warfare.

In the December 2018 article Inside China's Audacious Propaganda Campaign, authors Louisa Lim and Julia Bergin wrote extensively on how China was using media as a propaganda tool throughout the world. One such paragraph paints the picture:

> *"Since 2003, when revisions were made to an official document outlining the political goals of the People's Liberation Army, so-called "media warfare" has been an explicit part of Beijing's military strategy."*

One would not think that managing what your child did online would impact global politics. Certainly, one child has no impact. However, 600 million children providing both their demographic and psychographic information to a foreign government very well might be part of a new era of war and propaganda.

Tik Tok, Snapchat, Instagram, Twitch and YouTube all have their places in the world of your child. But those too will change and be replaced by another shiny new object that gains the attention of this generation.

But at this point, you're probably thinking, "My DiscMan, Palm Pilot and Nintendo 64 are looking pretty good about now."

THIRTEEN

How and Why Our Private Information is Invaded

I n 2017, I likely became the last person on earth to convert to Windows 10. It's not that I haven't tried. In fact, on two occasions I tempted fate and transitioned our three-year-old desktop to Windows 10, only to discover that my system crashed each time. Try as I might, our trusty ASUS desktop would have none of it.

However, my work laptop was quite another story. During our recent technology refresh, I was issued a brand-spanking new HP laptop running Windows 10. I love it. It's smart, fast and easy to learn. Although it has this obnoxious assistant, Cortana, who seems to be always stalking me. I've learned to live with her, or him or whatever.

The system is also quite inquisitive, always asking for information under the pretense of being service-oriented. Why all the questions? Unlike the guidance given in the movie The Graduate, the answer is not "Plastics." Rather, the answer is, "data."

But Microsoft is hardly the lone wolf roaming the digital plains. No, every application and social media platform lives, breathes and relies on data for its existence. We live in the economy of free.

Not really.

There is a price for everything we do on an app. As a wise man once said, "If it's free, you are the product."

Although this is true – it does not mean paid services won't "borrow" your data. For example, I've never received a free product from Amazon, but they likely know more about me than my wife. They have my data. Data is power.

However, you get the point. We are always exchanging our private information in return for the use of an app or service, or simply for convenience. There is a cost for providing free email, operating systems, and open access to friends, and free search engines. The business model requires the collection, analysis, and sale of your data.

13.1 Data Versus Metadata

I know, you've heard me use the term data and metadata. Are they interchangeable? Not really. In fact, there is an important differentiator.

Metadata is the data that defines the data.

For example. You take a picture with your phone. Behind that picture is metadata that includes the size of the file, the time at which it was taken, the luminance and saturation of the photo, the shutter speed and F-Stop and often the location in which you were standing. You can learn a lot by just viewing the metadata through a metadata reader.

So, without even seeing the photo, you might know where the person was when taking the picture and at what time. You'll also know the model of the phone. You can imagine how many crimes are solved just by seeing the metadata.

Data, on the other hand, usually refers to the physical content of a file. In our picture example, the physical image would contain the data. What was once a beautiful landscape is converted into a binary form of 0's and 1's to create a picture the human eye can see.

If it were a Word document, real words are converted to 0's and 1's and then, through an application, you can view the content. That is the data.

The date, time, word count, etc., make up the metadata.

Such metadata makes it easy for us to find data. It also helps law enforcement find people.

Let's say a robbery occurred at Eden Park in Cincinnati, Ohio. A suspect is caught the next day, and his phone is confiscated. The suspect swears he was not at Eden Park the evening of the robbery. His phone is inspected, and there are no photos from that day. However, there are text messages and phone calls made at the time of the crime.

By looking at the phone records, text messages, and other information, a treasure trove of metadata will reveal that the suspect was indeed at Eden Park at the time of the crime.

Although there is no photographic evidence, metadata paints a precise picture of the time and whereabouts of the suspect including any phone numbers he called, websites he's visited or to whom he sent a text message. In short, metadata is data about data.

Tag a photo: That is metadata.

Create a music category called "country." That is metadata.

Click a "hate" emoji about this book: that is sad—but it is also metadata.

Write an editorial about this book: that is data.

13.2 Data Stalkers

Regardless of what you're doing on Facebook or your child does on Snapchat or Instagram, or other apps, every move you make is being monitored, analyzed and then bundled with others for sale.

Let's say you traveled from San Francisco via Delta Airlines to Cincinnati, Ohio for a business meeting. When you arrive at the Cincinnatian Hotel, you log into their Wi-Fi. You collapse on the bed and check your Facebook feed. You see a picture of your sister's baby and click a LOVE emoji.

You scroll down and read a link about your least favorite politician. You click an angry emoji. Later, you read an article about the newest SUV to hit the market.

You scroll through your TV GUIDE App and browse what shows are on network and cable TV. You click a few to expand the show's information. You read about Game of Thrones, VEEP, and Silicon Valley.

Before you shower for dinner, you browse through ESPN.com to check the scores, and later view several other sites related to music, camping, and craft beer.

Following your shower, you access your UBER app for a ride to Cincinnati's Over the Rhine district. You visit friends at the Rook and Revel OTR before heading to the Reds' game at Great American Ballpark on the Cincinnati Bell Connector Street Car.

You finish the night with a quick beer at the Lager House before grabbing another UBER ride to your hotel, so that you are fresh for the morning meeting.

Sounds like a good evening. Other than your friends, the Uber driver, your waiters, and bartenders, few know you or anything about your travels for the day. In reality, everything you did was captured by either your smartphone, apps or all of the above.

When metadata is aggregated and analyzed, marketers know where you live and where you travel. In our scenario, they know you like craft beer and SUVs. Based on your browsing of TV shows, they know your entertainment preferences and age, and other demographic information.

They know you are likely close to your family because you clicked the LOVE emoji of your sister's baby.

They know your politics because of the hate emoji you clicked when reading a political article.

They know you probably like camping, music and craft beer due to the various websites you visited.

Given that you visited friends in Cincinnati's Over the Rhine, they know you're likely somewhat trendy – and also a baseball fan based on your trip to see the Reds play.

Each item of metadata that is captured, on its own, is practically useless. However, when aggregated, you have a multi-dimensional picture of who you are. There is a real financial value when millions of people's metadata with similar demographics are bundled and sold to data brokers. That is why data and metadata are so necessary. This is why understanding the various means given to protect your private information are so important.

Still not convinced?

Let's take a look at one popular teen app: Instagram.

About two years ago, attorney Adam Remsem, in a PetaPixel article, examined the Terms of Use Agreement for Instagram. Let's face it, few if anyone takes the time to read such legal jargon and any explanation would be helpful. He goes into great detail as to what we give up when we click, "I agree" to their Terms of Service Agreement. I recommend you read his article.

The 2019 version of the user agreement has changed somewhat but the spirit is still the same.

Yet simply reading the first paragraph of Instagram's Terms of Use should be cause for alarm:

> "Instagram does not claim ownership of any Content that you post on or through the Service. Instead, you hereby grant to Instagram a non-exclusive, fully paid and royalty-free, transferable, sub-licensable, worldwide license to use the Content that you post on or through the Service, subject to the Service's Privacy Policy, available here http://instagram.com/legal/privacy/, including but not limited to sections 3 ("Sharing of Your Information"), 4 ("How We Store Your Information"), and 5 ("Your Choices About Your Information"). You can choose who can view your Content and activities, including your photos, as described in the Privacy Policy."

You might pay particular attention to the words, *"you hereby grant to Instagram a non-exclusive, fully paid and royalty-free, transferable, sub-licensable, worldwide license to use the Content that you post on or through the Service..."*

Snapchat is similar. For example, in their 2019 Terms of Use, "Rights You Grant Us" section, they provide the following:

> "For all content you submit to the Services other than Public Content, you grant Snap Inc. and our affiliates a worldwide, royalty-free, sublicensable, and transferable license to host, store, use, display, reproduce, modify, adapt, edit, publish, and distribute that content. This license is for the limited purpose of operating, developing, providing, promoting, and improving the Services and researching and developing new ones.

What? I thought everything disappeared?"

Those are just a few of the things we give up when we use Instagram or Snapchat. But let's not be too hard on those apps, since others such as Facebook (which owns Instagram) Tik-Tok (formerly Musical.ly and Live.ly), WhatsApp, Tinder, Yubo (formerly Yellow) and every other free app tends to demand similar things from its users.

This might not seem important to you now. But what if your child's spring break photo that was posted on Instagram becomes the promotion for the Girls Gone Wild 2020?

Will that happen? Probably not.

Could it happen?

Absolutely.

13.3 You've Gone Viral

Several years ago, that realization occurred to Caitlin Seida, who retold her story in a Salon article titled My Embarrassing Picture Went Viral.

According to Seida, she decided to dress up like female superhero Laura Croft for Halloween. Ms. Seida has a medical condition that has made her overweight most of her life. However, being confident in her own skin, she threw caution to the wind and went out and celebrated Halloween like thousands of others.

Following the party, she posted a picture of herself on Facebook – which by her own admission was not flattering. What resulted was a tsunami of negative comments aimed at body shaming her.

Seida said:

"So, I laughed it all off at first — but then, I read the comments. What a waste of space," read one. Another: "Heifers like her should be put down." Yet another said I should just kill myself "and spare everyone's eyes." Hundreds of hateful messages, most of them saying that I was a worthless human being and shaming me for having the audacity to go in public dressed as a sexy video game character. How dare I dress up and have a good time!"

Sadly, these are the types of character assassinations you'd expect to read on a teen's post, not an adult's. However, her feelings were likely much like that of a teen who had just experienced the wrath of the queen bees of the school.

She went on to describe her feelings:

"We all know the awful humiliation of a person laughing at you. But that feeling increases tenfold when it seems like everyone is laughing at you. Scrolling through the comments, the world imploded — and took my heart with it."

As she readily admits in the article, she failed to set her security settings to private. That meant anyone wishing to look would have access to her picture. However, similar to Instagram, Facebook could have provided the picture to any of its partners for any purpose—causing just as much body shaming, perhaps more.

Would Facebook attempt to body shame Seida? Absolutely not! But how does Facebook know how the images they share with their 'partners' will be used? They don't. But their Terms of Use Agreement gives little indication of what they might do to or with any image, video or word you post.

FOURTEEN

Anything but Social

The most miserable example of how social media can unravel privacy and a life surfaced in January 2019, on the steps of the Lincoln Memorial in Washington DC. Three diverse groups gathered in front of the Lincoln Memorial with differing objectives. The result was a digital Rorschach test in the form of several videos related to the same subject. Everyone saw the videos through a different lens.

The first group was part of an African American religious organization known as the Black Hebrew Israelites, a group of Black Americans who believe they are descendants of the ancient Israelites.

The second, a group of high school boys from Covington Catholic, a Kentucky school just across the river from Cincinnati, Ohio. They had just attended the annual Right to Life walk and were waiting for their bus.

The third, a group of American Indians celebrating their heritage and finishing their Indigenous Peoples March on the steps of the Lincoln Memorial.

What ensued was a horrific cascade of verbal attacks and doxing of children and adults. These three divergent cultures — each armed with smartphones with cameras and microphones, captured the activity so they might feed their individual followers.

Allow me to digress for a moment.

Many years ago, if you wanted news, you turned to one of three broadcast news outlets: ABC, NBC or CBS. If one of these networks didn't report on a story, essentially, the story never happened. Twentieth Century Fox didn't launch the FOX Broadcast Network until 1985.

If you lived in one of the top fifty media markets, you likely had at least one major newspaper or more. Regardless, your news choices were still limited by the number of networks or papers that provided morning and evening news. If something happened at 2:00 p.m., you didn't know about it until the 6:00 p.m. network news.

Then in 1980, with the introduction of a twenty-four-hour news network called CNN, competition for eyeballs started to increase. Suddenly, stories that never had made it on broadcast networks such as *"95-year-old grandma wins surfing competition"* were being seen by cable subscribers.

Other competitors such as USA Today launched in September 1982. Fox Cable News launched three years later. These networks and newspapers competed with additional news outlets such as MSNBC, BuzzFeed, Drudge Report and thousands of podcasts. News, or what was sold as news, was available hours per day, often reported in the flavor most desired by their viewers or readers.

All these organizations—which are 'for-profits' businesses—are competing for the same ad dollars. So, to generate more money, they must find more eyeballs. Often, these reporters can't wait to run a story for the evening news. Today, news is delivered in real-time. Providers no longer report for the general population — they report what their beasts desire. If they don't give their audience what they want, they'll go elsewhere. In operating so, these national networks report from a political bent. In short, they report to feed their beasts.

Let's face it, Fox News and most radio talk shows report for conservatives. CNN, MSNBC and USA Today lean left – each feeding their own constituents which are their bread and butter. Stories are often formed before they are researched. They need to provide red meat to the beast. This week was no different.

White teen boys wearing MAGA hats are red meat for certain news organizations.

Conversely, young women wearing "pussy" hats last year during the Women's March were red meat for Fox News.

What has driven issues to their height today is the cesspool known as social media.

No doubt social media is a wonderful place to see how Aunt Gladys is doing in New Jersey, but it's sadly also a despicable tool for those who want to denigrate anyone with an opinion other than their own.

With that in mind, the January 2019 story was fodder for a digital disaster that would gain global coverage beyond anything I had ever witnessed concerning teenagers. Moreover, in doing so, it pointed to the power of words and images, digitally-captured, edited and distributed across Twitter, Facebook, Instagram, Snapchat and, of course, the aforementioned media outlets who eagerly snatched the videos from social media and reported on the events as factual news.

Today, everyone with a smartphone is an amateur photo-journalist capturing and editing that which best represents their own perspectives. This "event" resulted in a ninety-minute clash of cultures carefully edited down to a ninety-second portrait of something far bigger and complicated than most would admit.

For nearly ten years, I have spoken about the good, the bad, and the ugly of social media. Even in my wildest dreams, I never would have imagined how the dark underbelly of hatred—on all sides of the aisle —would unfold on a global scale in the name of money and politics. This was driven by cable news' unquenchable thirst for a crisis and social media trolls looking for an outlet to spew their anger. Left in the wake is the privacy of those involved. This could not have occurred without 7x24 cable TV news and social media.

However, what most disgusted me were the actions of adults, celebrities and "real journalists" suggesting that harm and even death should befall the students from Covington Catholic. The doxing of children and their families by some powerful adults is repulsive and despicable. Lives are at risk and the photos and videos tagged with these students' names will live in perpetuity.

The school was closed for a few days after the event. Threats of a school shooting, bombings and individual killings were being taken seriously.

The young man who is seen in the video as Mr. Phillips plays his drum mere inches from his face, has had his name and image broadcast throughout the world. He has become the Richard Jewell of our era.

Jewell was a security guard who found a knapsack that he felt might contain a bomb during the 1996 Atlanta Olympics. He alerted the Georgia Bureau of Investigation who then began clearing the area. The knapsack exploded minutes later, killing two people and injuring 111 others. Jewell's attentiveness spared hundreds of lives but could have been the worst disaster in Olympic history.

Sadly, Jewell became the main suspect when the headlines of the Atlanta Journal Constitution read: *FBI suspects 'hero' guard may have planted bomb.*

Much like we see all too often today, the newspaper had found Jewell hands-down guilty before the facts were available. Fortunately, Eric Rudolph was later found to be the perpetrator. However, not before Richard Jewell's life was all but ruined.

Google Richard Jewell and you'll find nearly 11 million links to his story. If you had Googled the young man's name from Covington Catholic following the news, you would have found nearly 6 million links in just four days. Today in July 2019, there were 2.7 million links. I will not use the young man's name out of respect for his family and his age—and because I don't also wish to add to his problem!

The fact that legitimate news outlets ran with this story before investigating is a testament to the state of 'journalism' on both the left and the right. Moreover, it is an example of the power of social media. Since everyone has a camera and a social media account, so-called news seems to happen in real time without regard for news ethics, contemplation or accuracy. Privacy be damned.

I'm in high schools every day. I've seen kids at their best and at their worst. That said, I jumped to conclusions against the boys when the story first hit. The alleged "crime" by the students seemed very possible to me, not because they were a Catholic school of primarily white young men but because they were KIDS! Kids sometimes do stupid things.

However, when I saw all the phones recording the incident in the initial short video, I did a search on YouTube to see if others had posted from different angles. There were several longer versions showing what happened before the confrontation with Mr. Phillips.

Why didn't some cub reporter take the time to search? Why didn't a news director or editor insist on different angles? There are at least a dozen on YouTube alone.

Why? If you must ask, the answer is generally money. Time is money. Get the story out before the competition. Feed the beast! Serve your political master.

Social media's success is becoming its demise.

Everyone's a reporter. Everyone is a photo journalist.

Everyone is an editor.

Everyone has a social media account.

Social media—and media in general—is proving to be anything but social.

Anyone who thinks these high school kids are all angels knows nothing about teens. I'm sure there may have been a few expletives volleyed in the direction of the Black Hebrew group. In the eyes of Mr. Phillips, some of them might have been disrespectful. But does anyone really think this situation and global outrage is warranted?

Be honest with yourself. How would you fare in a world where everything you do is captured? I know I would have failed that test when I was sixteen years old.

We live in a world where everything is being captured. From Ring video doorbells, to smartphones, to cameras blanketing entire cities. Most everything you or your child does might be recorded, edited and distributed across social media and news networks that need to feed the beast. Privacy is a thing of the distant past.

After seeing how this situation went viral, I immediately thought of what will inevitably happen in the near future. A technology called deepfakes allows users to take real-life human activities, i.e., stealing from a store, breaking and entering, or pornography, and replace the face in the original footage with that of another person. The results are often undetectable.

Prepare for deepfakes to be a challenge for all of us in the near future. If you think the activity in January 2019 in Washington, DC activities set the world aflame, you ain't seen nothing yet.

That said, I couldn't help but consider the irony of the last few words carved into the Lincoln memorial when we visited Washington DC with one of our grandkids in April, 2019:

"With malice toward none; with charity for all; with firmness in the right, as God gives us to see the right, let us strive on to finish the work we are in; to bind up the nation's wounds; to care for him who shall have borne the battle, and for his widow, and his orphan – to do all which may achieve and cherish a just and lasting peace, among ourselves, and with all nations."

We've got a long way to go.

14.1 Privacy: the Carbon Monoxide of the Internet?

Privacy is the stealth attacker. It is seldom seen or heard. It's the carbon monoxide of the Internet era, a fact of life in the Adolescent Tribal World State

I often ask students or parents attending our presentation on social media, "What if after 911, President Bush mandated that every American be injected with a chip that followed their every movement, conversation, and location? How would you have responded?"

The answer, of course, is with great indignation and rage. However, the government didn't exercise such plans, nor would they need to.

A few years later, our adoption of the smartphone made the issue a moot point. Today, most Americans are as attached to their devices as they are to their limbs. It's the first thing they see in the morning and the last thing they see at night.

Americans depend on smartphones to wake them, entertain them, direct them, answer perplexing questions and—yes, at times—speak to them. All of this happened following the introduction of the iPhone in 2007.

The physical and psychological price we have paid for such addictions include neck and back problems, hand and elbow issues, poor eyesight, and, of course, that permanent stooped downward stare that seems a benchmark of every connected youth. Yet, we seldom stop to consider the privacy issues technology has brought upon us that don't involve the government or marketing companies.

In 2015, the extramarital affair site Ashley Madison was hacked, and the private information of its members threatened to be released if the location was not shut down.

Troy Hunt, who runs the site "Have I Been Pwned?", revealed the Ashley Madison site flaw on Monday, July 20th, 2015. A weakness in the site exploited its email database which allowed hackers to determine if someone may have registered for an account on the site.

What is the result for many American spouses? Well... as Ricky Ricardo often said to Lucy, "You've got a lot of 'splaining to do!"

14.2 Data Breaches

You would think by now, most of us would understand there is no guarantee of privacy in a world dominated by technology and interconnected digital infrastructure. In fact, approximately fifty data breaches of prominent companies or apps are listed on "Have I Been Pwned?" Many of us use these resources daily, including Adobe, Snapchat, Forbes, Yahoo, Dominos, Sony, Vodafone and Minecraft Pocket Edition.

Does this mean every cretin, thief, thug, and miscreant is attempting to secure your information or that of your child? Of course not. But it does mean that you, your child and your information are easier to track than you might think.

Once that information is obtained—including just an email address —sites such as Spokeo can track all of your public social media accounts, home ownership information and much more for a few dollars per month.

Oftentimes, parents think the likelihood of their child's data being compromised is very small. However, as the chart below indicates, that type of thinking is not correct.

Experian published statistics suggesting that 31% of data breach victims later have their identity stolen. When you consider how many data breaches occur each year, this should be alarming to each of us. Then keep in mind, your child's personal data has at times been highjacked as well. Just Google "Instagram data breach", or "Tik Tok fine" and you'll see much of your child's information might already be in the ethers of the Internet.

I started this book in 2019. Between that time and the end of August 2019, there have been at least 4 billion records, which include such things as credit card numbers, home addresses, phone numbers and other highly sensitive information, stolen and exposed.

According to SelfKey , the following breaches occurred just in the two-month period of July 1st, 2019 through August 29th.

- 14 Million – Hostinger, August 25, 2019
- 1 Million – Suprema, August 14, 2019
- 23 Million – CafePress, August 5, 2019
- 50 Million – Poshmark, August 1, 2019
- 100 Million – Capital One, July 29, 2019
- 300,000 – QuickBit, July 22, 2019
- 5 Million – Bulgaria's National Revenue Agency, July 17, 2019
- 14,600 – Los Angeles County Department of Health Services, July 10, 2019
- 78,000 – Maryland Dept. of Labor, July 6, 2019
- Mars Mission Data – NASA, June 24, 2019

14.3 Privacy in the Workplace

Those working at large companies understand that often, corporate Human Resources departments might monitor them through key cards and video cameras. Additionally, the infrastructure provided by corporate IT registers each login of laptops or tablets, including keystrokes, email, and web browsing.

However, whether in the home, at the office or otherwise, if you're using a corporate device, understand that you might be under the watchful eye of HR.

The Case of Darek Kitlinski

The same might be true for those working for our federal government. Yes, I know your child is not working for the CIA, Social Security or the White House. But this is relevant for the ADT and adults.

Take the case of Darek Kitlinski, who claims he was refused a transfer within the DEA due to his status as a Coast Guard reservist. Friction grew between him and his superior over the issue.

According to reporter Lee Ross of Fox News, after leaving a secure DEA garage, Darek noticed a red blinking light coming from under the hood of his SUV. He reached in and pulled out a still functioning Blackberry bearing a DEA identification sticker.

The device allegedly traced back to the DEA's top Human Resources officer. It's worth noting that nowadays, technological advances and the affordability of 'useful' malware means many employers are routinely installing spyware on employees' devices, and trackers are covertly attached to employees' cars.

This makes it simple to determine if someone is really sick or whether the delivery boy does deliver the pizza, in addition to the employer having access to everything the employee does with their work laptop or phone.

It costs under $20 per month to run a covert tracker on a vehicle, and around $200 per annum for a third party to track every keystroke, see every image, monitor every chat, etc., on a laptop or phone. Worse still, once your child's phone becomes infected with spyware, this will likely self-propagate through the whole network of your child's contacts so then every child is placed at risk.

While these are unusual situations and may not apply to our kids, it's important to note that the world of communication has changed and will continue to alter the methods we use to communicate private information. Privacy is no longer guaranteed and corporate 'investigation' often traverses the fuzzy boundaries of ethics.

Given the abilities of today's smartphones to record video and audio and to track locations, imagine the consequences when they are used against individuals who think the information is private.

Below are just a couple of real-life scenarios that appeared in the news:

- A student confronts a teacher who had sexually abused her. Their phone conversation is recorded on her smartphone.
- A journalist records her false confessions to various priests and then broadcasts them.
- A worker is fired, and the meeting with HR is recorded.
- During an athletic practice, a coach is recorded verbally disciplining a player.
- Recording in a locker room when athletes are showering and changing.
- Recording of a conversation between doctors and nurses during surgery.
- Snapchatting by a surgeon during a breast augmentation of a patient.

14.4 When You Click Send

So, you might be thinking, this is all very interesting, but I need something with more meat. This won't happen to *my* kid. Right?

Well first, let me take you back a few decades. For centuries, there were few things more riveting or intimate than actual words, handwritten from the heart—to be read on paper. That's why so many of us can relate to the words of 'The Letter', famously sung by one of my favorite singers Joe Cocker.

It's hard to imagine old Joe singing:

Gimme a ticket for an airplane
Ain't got time to take a fast train
Lonely days are gone, I'm a-going' home
My baby just sent me a text.

The art of writing and the experience of finding in your mailbox, hand-written words of love and concern have long since vanished. But does this mean that today's words of love and concern expressed via a digital device using 140 characters should not be private?

There is likely no turning back the clock. Texting is often the new love letter of this generation. However, unlike twenty years ago, there is little means of controlling their distribution. Once your child clicks *send,* they have lost total control of their words, photos, and videos. Even the emojis they click are recorded.

This is all part of the marketing data being sold daily about your child, that we will discuss in our next chapter.

FIFTEEN

Your Child & Marketing Data

The Adolescent Tribal World State is like no other generation. They are the first generation to grow up with technology. They are also the first generation where much of what they have done or said, and where they have been and with whom, has been recorded, analyzed and then unashamedly sold.

As we have indicated throughout this book, we spend significant time worrying about our kids' involvement in sexting, bullying, ephemeral digital messages, and pornography. There should be equal concern about their privacy. We've discussed privacy in previous chapters, but it is important for us to better understand why you should be concerned.

There is a lack of control over your child's content and the metadata collected by the apps they use and the messages, pictures, and videos they post and send.

There's an entire industry trying to sell and buy our information. Much of this analysis of our data is done with the intent of marketing products to us based on the knowledge of our real interests. Sometimes, that makes our lives easier.

Many times, I have purchased books from Amazon based on their understanding of my likes and dislikes. However, as we have seen all too often following the Target, Home Depot and Sony hacks, there is no guarantee that our most intimate and private information will not be distributed to others and to the world.

Our challenge as individuals, businesses, and as a nation is to enjoy the conveniences of our digital lives while mitigating the risk of this data being unwittingly or purposely distributed. The adoption of the PC by businesses and consumers in the 1980s and then of the web in the 1990s seemed like an excellent migration to a faster and better world of communication. Few of us saw the unintended consequences of communicating on a global digital network. Moreover, who thought that this system and even smaller devices would be navigated by children in the 3rd and 4th grades, with many establishing online personas often without adult supervision? Certainly not me.

Just like a criminal on any number of the CSI TV shows, we leave evidence of our lives when we use a digital device. If you're online, you are giving up a little piece of who you are. It starts out rather small —for example, the IP address of your device—but grows larger as you surf the web, fill out online forms, download apps, search words, or move from one location to another throughout the day—or any other activity. In that way, it's much like a detective gathering evidence. It starts with something small but as more evidence is collected, it allows the person or system analyzing the data or metadata to construct a complete picture of who you are, where you go, and with whom you associate.

This information can be used by individual companies or sold to third-party organizations. While that might seem like a small price to pay to have access to such robust apps like Google, YouTube Fortnite, Minecraft, and others, what happens when we are using that technology, or those apps and websites?

15.1 Cookies

Most of us have heard of those tiny pieces of digital code called cookies. They have been around since the early 1990s. They're one of those little annoyances of our digital life. How do they work? Well, when you visit many websites, they'll often place cookies related to your visit onto your hard drive.

These seemingly innocent pieces of code might include information related to your login or registration identification, user preferences, online "shopping cart" information, and so on.

Sometimes, the info is there only to make the page load faster, or to make it easier for you to find information of interest. But as I mentioned earlier, sometimes this data is sold to third parties. This is why that new fishing rod you viewed on the Pro-Bass website seems to follow you on ESPN, the New York Times and San Francisco Chronicle websites.

You might also know that over time, the collection of such cookies slows down the processing of the device. When this happens, go to your mobile or laptop settings and delete these annoying – yet sometimes helpful pieces of code.

15.2 Metadata, Data, and Your Mobile Device

You might think using a mobile device makes it easier to secure your privacy. However, you'd be wrong. With mobile devices, we use apps rather than simply surfing the web. Apps often collect significant amounts of private information and send such data to the app developer and even to third parties. This applies especially to the so-called free apps.

What metadata might be collected by an app? Well, you might be surprised. As I mentioned in an earlier chapter, Facebook has ninety-eight data points about each user, including:

- Your call logs
- Your location
- Your personal contacts
- Your calendar information
- Your internet data
- Your unique IDs
- Information about how you use the app itself
- Your email platforms

Maybe you're the kind of person that believes technology has corrupted an entire generation and life was better in the 1980s. Hey! There's nothing wrong with the 1980s other than the music and all of that big hair. The reality is that the era of big hair ushered in the ubiquitous corporate use of email.

As consumers began to adopt the web in the 1990s, email grew precipitously. Perhaps you remember those now famous words from your first AOL account, *You've Got Mail.*

That first AOL account allowed us to send messages across the world to our dearest friends, relatives and perhaps our mortal enemies. They even made a movie about it by the same name. What could possibly go wrong there?

Well, we know that answer.

General David Petraeus had his Gmail hacked, revealing an affair that brought his once heralded career to a stunning end.

The Sony hack revealed thousands of personal and business emails that subsequently brought to a halt the distribution of a multi-million-dollar movie titled, The Interview.

Eventually, Sony released the movie to about 300 theaters on December 23rd in 2014. In a somewhat unique twist, the movie was also available to users of Google Play, Xbox Video, and YouTube before the end of that month.

And of course, there was the Hillary Clinton email scandal of 2016. Is that still going on? Probably.

Most of us know that when we correspond through email, we are giving information to the recipient that can be used to support or destroy us. However, you might *also* be providing information to any number of people, including your employer, the government, your e-mail provider, and anyone with whom your recipient chooses to share the message. An unencrypted e-mail message can potentially be seen by anyone while that communication is in transit. If sent from an employer-owned device, it could be read by your employer too.

If you use a webmail service such as Gmail or Yahoo, your emails could be scanned by the webmail provider. This is done to both sort and detect spam and to better deliver appropriate ads to your account.

For example, Gmail scans incoming emails and places relevant advertisements next to the e-mail. Yahoo Mail performs different but somewhat similar scanning of email content.

Today's reality is that we need to be aware of the risks involved in any communication using a digital device and network.

15.3 Your Child's Apps

Apps often share your information with the developer of the app, including your general location. Be aware that a free app is always free for a reason. Read the "Terms of Use" and "Privacy Policy" before downloading any app to your device.

Personal information on your social media sites is accessed by search engines such as Google and Bing. The best way to keep this data and metadata from finding its way into the hands of others is to lock your security setting to 'private' or 'friends only'.

Even then, you have no control what your friends might do with your posts. Moreover, the app owner still has access to all your personal information.

Although most adults don't use Snapchat, Kik, WhatsApp, Whisper, Sarahah, and other youth-oriented apps but your children probably do. Each service publishes its Terms of Service that few people read when they opt into the app.

For example, in Snapchat's Privacy agreement they state:

Usage Information:
We collect information about your activity and the messages you send and receive through our Services. For example, we collect information such as the time, date, sender, recipient of a message, the number of messages you exchange with your friends, which friends you exchange messages with the most, and your interactions with messages (such as when you open a message or capture a screenshot). We may collect that same basic information when you use Snapcash, along with the dollar amounts sent and received.

Information Collected by Cookies and Other Tracking Technologies:
Like most online services, we use cookies, web beacons, and other technologies. Cookies are small data files stored on your hard drive or in device memory that

store information about your use of the Services, which can, among other things, help us see which areas and features of the Services are popular and let us count visits".

There are many other items in their agreement that anyone using the service should read before using.

15.4 Return of the Bots

Scenario: Your child is endlessly staring at the small rectangular screen, eyebrows arched as if anxiously awaiting the revelation of life's greatest mystery from the furtive party on the other side of the screen.

She giggles with delight and then laughs loudly followed by the words, "I can't believe you said that to me!"

Concerned that some vapid juvenile delinquent just disparaged your daughter, you grab the phone to digitally break his face when you realize the aberrant offender is not a person but rather the Magic Eight Bot. Magic Eight Bot? What?

Yep, the round black ball of our youth is now an active bot on Kik, a popular messaging app used by nearly 40% of American teens. However, Magic Eight is just one of many bots on Kik and other apps, with thousands more being developed and available on apps such as Facebook, Snapchat, and others.

15.5 What Exactly is a Bot or Chatbot?

According to Matt Schlicht, CEO of Octane AI & Founder of Chatbots Magazine:

"A chatbot is a service, powered by rules and sometimes artificial intelligence, that you interact with via a chat interface. The service could be any number of things, ranging from functional to fun, and it could live in any major chat product (Facebook Messenger, Slack, Telegram, Text Messages, etc.)"

You probably use them a lot but didn't know classification name. It could be an automated weather forecast or a voice system used for ordering food online.

Alexa and Siri are bots. If you think back to your hazy, crazy days of college, you might recall AOL's Instant Messenger known as SmarterChild. Well, they've come a long way since SmarterChild, and they're getting smarter.

So, why do teens find them so compelling?
In some respects, because this generation's preferred means of communication can be summed up in two separate words: "Mobile" and "Messaging."

Additionally, flying under the radar for most of us is the growth of Artificial Intelligence or AI. These developments and the evolution and popularity of messaging platforms, such as Facebook Messenger, WhatsApp, WeChat, and Viber are energizing this new age of meaningful interaction with bots and chatbots.

According to eMarketer, there are 1.4 billion monthly users on messaging platforms each spending about twenty-three minutes and twenty-three seconds a day chatting.

For marketers, that is a potential goldmine.
Just like "bricks and mortar" retailers want you to spend more time in their stores, marketers want you to spend more time with bots because it can lead to higher product sales.

Who is at the epicenter of this change? You guessed it – your child, aka Gen Z.

Consider the Stats: Collectively, the top four messaging apps that we mentioned above have more registered users, higher retention, and higher engagement than the top four social networks. Change is not happening… it already took place when we were not looking.

So, are social media apps going away? Although the trend of downloading new apps is slowing, it does not mean that Instagram, Facebook, Twitter and others are going away anytime soon. However, it does suggest the tsunami of new apps might be a thing of the past as more and more people are settling on the use of approximately five apps. Additionally, you already see apps such as Facebook, Snapchat and Instagram morphing into messaging apps, banks and the like.

Additionally, organizations such as Facebook are at the forefront of bot development – adding many to their platforms. Venture Beat reports that Facebook developers have created more than 11,000 chatbots for its Messenger platform. The aforementioned Kik platform —which internationally is a top teen messaging app—now has over 6,000 new chatbots.

Remember, the reason apps, and now bots exist is to sell something in one of two ways:

- To *convince you* to buy a product under the auspices of providing free, helpful information

Or,

- To sell *your* information to a marketing company.

The advantage for marketing businesses and developers is that bots can circumvent App Store approval, updates, and a user's operating system. Additionally, bot development is easier to execute.

Since the very profitable youth culture spends so much of their time with messaging apps, bots are often the best means of connecting with this demographic.

As Todd Dean, co-founder and chief marketing officer at the mobile-first employment solution Wirkn wrote in Venture Beat:

"Chatbots are fun and exciting today, and teens are the main barometer and the ones to watch as they engage and drive the evolution. Companies that fund chatbot development are taking notice and voting with their wallets. There is no question in my mind that chatbots are here to stay and that they will play a very big role in the future of innovation. They may just become so human-like and ubiquitous that we don't even know they are there."

Although there are thousands of new bots embedded in apps and websites, most are rather non-threatening to your child. Yet parents and guardians must understand that with every great technology advancement, there is often inappropriate content developed around such technology. We, of course, have seen this over the years with pornography. With the proliferation and easy access to Internet porn, addiction has become an issue for children as young as twelve. Sadly, as we've seen in the past, we now see porn bots embedded in some of the apps our kids use.

Are BOTS really spewing porn to our kids? According to a 2014 article in Forbes, writer Parmy Olson said:

"These are fake, autonomous programs that more often than not, try to entice Kik's users to click on paid-for sites with flirty conversations and the promise of porn—glorified chat bots with one thing in mind

.According to Kik, "porn bots" make up around 1% of the app's entire message volume each day, suggesting that thousands of them regularly crawl its network."

Much of bot porn is solicited through spamming. Olson also suggested,

"The spammers may be in this for the long haul because they're making good money."

Given the vulnerability of teens and their sometimes access to their parents' credit card information, this is also a potentially expensive issue for families.

Ironically, ONWARD is a new bot to help minimize our addictions to pornography and additions to screen time, dating apps, shopping, gambling and video games.

Naturally, most kids are not speaking with porn bots. So what bots are they using?

According to Chatbot Magazine, (Yes that's a thing) the following are the best bots on the market:

- Mitsuku - Information
- Rose - Information
- Right Click -Website Creation
- Poncho - Weather

- Insomno – Sleep Help
- Dr. A.I – Health Symptom Checker
- Meldoy by Baidu - Health

Last year, TechJunkie had a warning concerning a very popular app called Sensay:

"Sensay matches you up with a complete stranger to chat about anything. It can use location to find another Kik user close by or further away and is an excellent way to meet new people anonymously. The bot will not identify your username so you actually can chat about absolutely anything. Sometimes, this will work in your favor, other times it actually won't!"

When they say anything… they mean anything.

So, take heed, Mom and Dad. Is it better that your son or daughter is being wooed or affronted by a stranger on Kik, Snapchat, Yellow, or Instagram, or by a bot storing information about their likes, dislikes, location, purchases, awake time, etc?

Remember your answer the next time your child says to her phone, "I can't believe you just said that to me."

15.6 Public Websites

We must understand that there is so much information about you already on public websites, such as the auditor of your county that provides detailed information about your home, its value, your mortgage and your county taxes.

When you combine this data and metadata with that available by searching social media, a treasure trove of information becomes available to anyone interested in learning more about you. One such service, Spokeo, aggregates your social media data with public information available on government sites.

For less than $10.00 per month, you can quickly research anyone. However, if you have all of your social media locked down to private or friends only, none of your social media information can be accessed. That is, of course, unless you have made comments on someone else's social media account that is not set on "private." Then, it is there for public consumption.

Additionally, any profile photo you have ever used on social media is available to be seen by anyone, even if you have the strictest privacy settings. As such, if you or your child has ever used a photo you wouldn't want your grandma or boss to see, delete it. Even the old ones.

15.7 Credit Cards & Metadata

Personal information is attached to each of your credit cards, some of which have RFID chips that can be read by anyone nearby with an RFID reader. You can't keep hackers from accessing your bank's files, but you can keep your credit cards secure by using RFID credit card protector sleeves. These small, lined credit card holders block RFID signals and add another layer of personal identity protection.

Digital technologies have changed the way we work, play and raise our families. For the most part, it's been a welcome evolution in our culture. But keeping track of these changes can be difficult.

Although most us will never need to deal with many of the scenarios I mentioned, our children must know that such misuse of technology among unscrupulous individuals can place obstacles to their education, careers, and relationships.

No other generation in our history has had to deal with such an evolution of technology and its impact on our private lives.

In today's environment, skilled (and at times unskilled) hackers can access smartphones externally to monitor their movements and even eavesdrop on conversations.

15.8 Smartphone Hacking on Public Wi-Fi

Although there are many ways your smartphone content might be compromised, most frequently this occurs when you use unsecured, public Wi-Fi.

During my presentation with teens, I show a video concerning how easy it is to hack their phones through a technique called spoofing.

This gets their attention since so many of them use Wi-Fi at Starbucks, McDonald's, Panera Bread and many other public establishments. It's not the fault of the restaurant or coffee shop. Rather, it's the trust that teens place in public Wi-Fi.

Just as in your home, public Wi-Fi provides what is called an SSID. This essentially is the name of the network you are about to access and log into. If you are a frequent visitor to Panera Bread, you might not know which SSID or Wi-Fi network is provided for customers. Is it the one labeled Panera, Panera Bread, Panera Free Wi-Fi? We don't always know.

But before we go further, understand that pedophiles and many miscreants prey on teens and tweens. They know their market!

- They know over 75% of teens have smartphones
- They know teens like to gather at restaurants and coffee shops
- They know teens access free Wi-Fi
- They know about 20-30% of teens have inappropriate photos or conversations on their devices.

Knowing these facts, the bad guy might hang out there as well, or in the parking lot. Using the "hot spot" capability of his device, he creates a fake Wi-Fi network that looks just like that offered by the restaurant or coffee shop.

When the teen decides to use the free Wi-Fi, he or she is presented with several options, all of which look legitimate. But what if they log into the wrong Wi-Fi? The answer: all of their photos and messages are copied without any of their knowledge.

If there are inappropriate images or videos, those are often traded with other bad guys or posted to child porn websites. The teen has no idea what just happened. By the way, this happens to adults as well.

How do we protect our children from all this invasion? That's what our next chapter covers.

SIXTEEN

Protecting Your Child's Private Information

W hat can you do to prevent unauthorized access to your child's data in this way? First and foremost, the user should never have inappropriate info on a smartphone. If you do have this, you are a target for such theft. However, if you can't help yourself, at least ask the manager of the establishment for the correct SSID.

However, consider these statistics:

According to the Internet Watch Foundation, 88% of inappropriate images find their way into the hands of those for whom they were not intended.

How does this happen? Often through hacks.

Additionally, never do important banking using public Wi-Fi. Although you are most likely not being hacked, it's best to do these things on networks that you know are secure.

Keep your smartphone and tablet's operating system updated. By doing so, you minimize your vulnerability to such attacks.

Consider using a VPN when doing anything outside of your network. Even then, it can help you circumvent privacy issues.

As Adi Sharabani, the co-founder of mobile security company Skycure, told CNBC's Jennifer Schlesinger in her 2016 article:

Your smartphone could be hacked without your knowledge.

"At the end of the day, everything is hackable. What I am surprised about is that people sometimes forget that it's so easy to hack into these devices."

As we have discovered in our own research, any Wi-Fi used at such places as airports, cafes, and restaurants can be unsecured, allowing the bad guy to view everything on your device while connected.

16.1 VPN's & Proxy Servers

OK, you've got everything locked down at home. You know all of the passwords for every device in the house. You've secured the iTunes and Google Play stores and are running every filter known to man. You're good, right?

Well... Recently, Opera, the web browser developed by Opera Software announced it would add a free VPN service to its latest version. This press release created a flood of questions about online privacy, VPNs and proxy servers.

What? You actually work for a living and are raising three kids who play sports, are on a dance team, and twice a week you need to drive them to tuba practice? Now you need to be even more vigilant? No worries. We've got your back!

16.2 What are VPNs?

VPNs, or virtual private networks, provide an added level of security when you're surfing the web using one of the top browsers. For example: If you're using a Mac, iPhone or iPad, you are probably using the default browser called Safari.

If you're using an Android device, you're probably using Chrome.

Windows laptops and desktops generally use Explorer or its newest iteration named Edge.

And still, others might be using Mozilla's Firefox or Amazon's Silk. All could, to some extent, provide surfing privacy.

16.3 Browser Privacy

Safari, Firefox and Amazon's Silk, privacy features are called 'Private Browsing'.

In Google Chrome it's called *Incognito*.

Explorer/Edge refers to this feature as *InPrivate Browsing*.

Opera not-so creatively refers to theirs as *Private Tab / Private Window*.

In essence, each one attempts to provide some level of privacy from advertisers and others interested in knowing your browsing information.

But hey! You don't want anyone sniffing around your digital world without a search warrant unless they're also carrying a gift card to Starbucks. What are your options? The answer very well might be the use of a VPN or perhaps a proxy server.

16.4 Tell Me More About VPNs

There are hundreds of VPNs from which to select. Some are free. Some charge a subscription fee. However, for this conversation, we'll address some of your free options.

As we mentioned, if you adopt the Opera browser on your laptop or desktop, you'll have a free VPN service. This allows you to surf the web without too much concern from snoopers. You can also access the foreign versions of services such as Netflix. However, this same technology also allows your child to circumvent some of the controls you've placed on your network.

For now, the service will only work on a laptop or desktop. However, future versions will be available for mobile devices.

Hola
Firefox offers the Hola or Hola Unblocker as a free VPN service. However, I've often had issues when adding certain plugins on Firefox. Although Firefox supposedly checks each plugin they offer, I have found them to sometimes have issues.

BetterNet

Google's Chrome allows Hola and other VPN services such as BetterNet. BetterNet is considered a quality service with an excellent reputation.

Both Hola and BetterNet are available for mobile devices as well. Most VPNs provide some great features, such as:

- Perhaps one of the biggest benefits is the protection they provide when using public Wi-Fi hotspots. These hotspots are often used by hackers searching for private data. VPNs can minimize the chance of a hacker accessing your information.
- Hiding IP addresses by masking a user's IP address with a virtual IP address. The result? It makes it more difficult for the sites you visit to track you.
- Unblocking firewalls and websites. In this case, the VPN allows users to bypass blocked sites by circumventing the network. This has been a huge issue for school networks.

In essence, VPNs helps to maintain your private communication by hiding your digital sessions from criminal elements. Or if you're a criminal, it can hide your activity from law enforcement!

VPNs are the equivalent of placing a small hose inside a larger hose. Both hoses are streaming water in the same direction, across the same property. However, the smaller stream is shielded from mixing with the other data.

In the case of your VPN protected data, it is not easily viewed by others on the same network.

However, don't be fooled into a false sense of security when using VPNs or proxy servers. Gold Frog wrote an excellent article a year or so ago when they did a detailed analysis of such strategies.

Any of these approaches should be used only as a safeguard against your private information being stolen. However, no system is perfect. No system is impenetrable from someone that knows what they're doing.

16.5 What the Heck is a Proxy Server?

Chances are, if your child uses a tablet or device on a school network, they are intimately familiar with proxy servers. Proxy servers are used to evade school networks so that students can legitimately access great training videos on YouTube, or in some cases, porn on other sites. A proxy server hands off a request to an authorized website by using another site's URL or address.

In such a case, the school's or business's network filters are fooled into thinking that the requested website is acceptable. The network then delivers the unacceptable but requested web content to the user.

Recently, the online site, Gleanster published a list of the top free proxy servers available. It's an interesting read that will give you an insight into how easy it can be to hide your identity or online activity.

They include:

- HideMyAss
- 4everproxy
- AnonyMouse
- proxysite.com
- whoer.net
- hide.me
- Kproxy
- BlewPass

When dealing with your kids, the best protection against them visiting an inappropriate website is by just talking to them about your concerns. Building trust between a parent and a child is sometimes a forgotten art. However, most students with whom I've spoken want that conversation.

Moreover, they want to build that trust.

However, I also have spoken to many parents in which cases, regardless of the strategies they took, their child attempted to undermine every policy. In those cases, please consider the parental controls listed by Consumeradvocate.org. Their 2019 top picks are:

- Bark
- NetNanny
- Securly://
- Qustodio
- Norton

16.6 Opera: The Italian Word for 'Work'

We started this discussion with news about the Opera browser. Interestingly, the art form we know as opera is considered the fusion of music, drama, visual arts, and dance. It's also the Italian word for 'work' and has a 400-year history in western civilization. It truly was an evolution in the world of the arts.

In the world of network technology, we too are seeing the development of digital technology as the 2020 world of mobile apps collides with the 1995 world of websites. Somewhere in between will be a new world for parents to master. For now, you're armed with what many of your kids already know.

It's difficult to digest and manage this change of technology. Or, as the Italians might say. *It's Opera.*

16.7 Facial Recognition

How many times have you uploaded photos to Facebook and thought, "how does this app know that pic is of weird Uncle Charlie?" Perhaps you wondered briefly and then went back to the business of uploading your child's birthday party pics, or last weekend's barbecue.

However, the reality is that Facebook is using a potent tool known as facial recognition software. In fact, many say that Facebook's actual facial recognition program is much more robust than that used by the FBI to catch every ne'er-do-well from here to Helsinki.

But what if someone were able to secure every picture associated with Facebook? Other than an absolute violation of your privacy, what harm could there be? The answer might surprise you. Why? Because if anyone had access to all of the social media photos and videos on apps such as Facebook, Instagram, Twitter, Tik Tok, Snapchat, etc. it would mean they'd have a window into your identity without having ever met you.

For example, Government uses facial recognition technology to catch the bad guys. However, twenty-six states use this same technology for everyone with a driver's license. This allows government agencies to quickly identify you – and identify anyone that has stolen your identity.

Maybe we're fine with our federal and local governments being able to identify us under the auspices of preventing identity theft. But what about social media companies? Should they have access to such power?

As suggested, Facebook's technology is better at identifying people through photos than the FBI. This is in part because Facebook has 1.65 billion users, each of whom posts hundreds, if not thousands, of pics each year. Therefore, their data sets are better and facial recognition learning becomes enhanced.

This is called machine learning.

But can someone steal your photos on social media? Today, if a user's account does not have the proper privacy settings, these pictures can be compromised and used for just about any purpose. In fact, you cannot secure your profile picture on any social media platform. They are open to the public.

To our knowledge, no one has been able to hack Facebook's entire collection of photos and associated metadata. However, someone has been able to access a dataset containing 40,000 images of both men and women from Tinder. Given that most of these photos are not of "the big 3", i.e., birthdays, bar mitzvahs or barbecues, the stakes are little higher for those whose images grace the digital vaults of Tinder.

Stuart Colianni wrote a program to compile Tinder photos, intending to use them for machine-learning research. His rationale: "Why not leverage Tinder to build a better, larger facial dataset?"

For his research, he added folders containing the photos to Google's Kaggle, a service that provides programmers the ability to experiment with artificial intelligence algorithms. Such algorithms can be focused on large photographic datasets to perform facial recognition tasks.

Well, as one might imagine, this upset the folks at Tinder – but not half as much as the college students, married doctors, lawyers, CPA's and other professionals and non-professionals whose alter-egos "were looking for love in all the wrong digital places."

So, what's the big deal? In short, as was reported in a Vocativ article:

> *"Strangers can use them to catfish others — the act of posing as a person to lure another. Internet strangers can also reverse-search nameless photos and potentially find who they belong to as well."*

Again, it's hard to compare Tinder's User Stats to those of Facebook's 1.65 billion users. But given the perspective mentioned by Vocativ above, imagine the damage that could be inflicted on Facebook users if every such photo became part of a sophisticated, Artificial Intelligence, and facial recognition database.

We must come to grips in this generation of algorithms, with the fact that our faces are nothing more than mathematics. In fact, the math that makes up our face never changes. As such, using sophisticated facial recognition technology, your high school picture could be scanned and subsequently find you on any number of social media platforms, five, ten, or thirty years after you graduated.

Surprised by all of this? Most people are. However, flying under the radar for most of us is Google's "Vision" and Amazon's new Image Recognition service called "Rekognition."

Yes, it's spelled with a K.

Amazon's service was launched in 2016 and according to their website:

> *"Rekognition API lets you quickly build powerful visual search and discovery into your applications. With Amazon Rekognition, you only pay for the images you analyze and the face metadata you store. There are no minimum fees, and there are no upfront commitments."*

Although this service won't help you hack Facebook or other social media apps, it will help you identify people in photos that you might take or have found elsewhere. There is a free tier that will help you understand how powerful facial recognition is—and where this technology might take us in the future.

Not everyone wants to pay for such services. In that case, there are reverse image look-up sites such as Tin Eye that can find identical images on the web by scraping social media sites to unearth the exact images you used for your search.

This is just the beginning.

Fortunately, the scraping of 1.65 billion user photos on Facebook did not happen this week. However, 40,000 Tinder users are wondering what disturbing images of them might be floating in the ethers of the Internet.

16.8 Social Listening & Your Child's Scholarship

A while back, I was visiting an Ohio high school to present our Social Media program to two different groups of high school students. While waiting for the second group to enter the auditorium, the football coach approached me and said, "I wish you had been here yesterday." I laughed and asked him, "Why?" He then went on to tell me how his number one player had just lost a $200,000 football scholarship to a Division I program, for sending one negative Tweet about a girl in the school.

Apparently, the young man didn't know that most Division I schools have staff that use social listening programs to monitor recruits and existing players on social media.

It used to be that the only way you could keep tabs on your recruits was from their high school coaches, school administration, the newspaper covering local sports and when allowed, periodic phone calls to the recruit. Those days have long since passed. Today, there's social listening.

Say what? Social Listening comes in a variety of forms. In some cases, it's simply a staff member in the athletic department who manually follows high school recruits and current players through their activity on Twitter, Instagram, or Facebook. For larger athletic departments, it's using such tools as GeoFeedia, SnapTrends and other tools that can literally follow hundreds or thousands of feeds from athletes on most any given social media platform. Schools that might spend $500,000 in tuitions and development of a player want to be certain the young man or woman is of good character and behavior. These tools are often a part of the litmus test.

In my travels, I've likely made the same observations as you. An 18-year-old boy or girl might look like an adult, but in many ways, they are still kids. Then consider that each one of them has a tool in their hand that provides instantaneous self-gratification through ephemeral texting, heavily-filtered selfies, hashtag-laden tweets and sentence-ending emojis. Even the best of teens often will say and do things without any thought of the consequences.

16.9 Lack of Empathy Makes Coaches Wonder

In her book, UnSelfie, Why Empathetic Kids Succeed In Our All-About Me World, Michele Borba, Ed.D., an internationally-renowned consultant, educational psychologist and recipient of the National Educator Award, studied this issue. She suggests that many teens are so obsessed with texting and "selfies" that they've never learned empathy for their peers and those in their homes and communities.

I think we have all been out to eat only to see a family of four with their noses buried in their phones without regard to the people at their table. The human social factor that helps to deliver empathy is often missing in today's youth.

The resulting "Selfie Generation" has indeed created an empathy crisis. In her book, Dr. Borba says that teens today are 40% less empathetic than they were just a generation ago, and narcissism has increased by a colossal 58%. Much like the boy that lost a scholarship for sending a nasty tweet about a girl at his school, our new digital culture has led to teens making rash judgments and taking quick action without regard to consequences.

There are countless examples of how a teen's digital actions have created enormous obstacles to their future success. It is often best witnessed during the recruiting season at high schools across the country.

The problem continues when the recruit enrolls in the college. Assistant IU basketball coach, J.D. Campbell told the Indy Star:

"It's just really important to be honest, and really important to remind them as much as you possibly can, that your reputation is always on the line. Break it down to them that this is your family, you represent your family first."

Your digital reputation can follow you for life; there's no taking back a Tweet, a post, a picture or a video. If it's on social media, it's now searchable.

Nebraska Director of Player Personnel Ryan Gunderson told ESPN that social media, *"Has revolutionized recruiting. Sure, cell phones have had a huge influence in the process, allowing recruiters to go mobile with their communication. But with today's technology, cell phones are merely a vehicle for social media use."*

Unfortunately, for every good, there is often a bad. Through social media, coaches can easily see what a recruit is posting, what they like or share, and have access to their social media friends.

In just a few minutes, a coach can decide an athlete's behavior and character. It might not be the reality but as they say, "perception is reality." You seldom have a chance to explain. In thirty seconds, you could be written off of a recruiting list due to your social media activity — and not even know it.

In the ESPN January 2016 RecruitingNation Article, Jeremy Crabtree wrote about SMU Defensive Coordinator Van Malone. Coach Van Malone tweeted a redacted dossier on one of the Mustangs' commitments. It's a tremendous insight into how coaches make decisions as it relates to a recruit's social media activity.

Social media can illustrate a student's work in the community, their academic and athletic accomplishments and their communication skills. Social media has infinite possibilities for those who master its positive use.

"I wish you had been here yesterday," resonates with me still today. How many young men and women were on the radar of a college but unbeknownst to them, they were dropped from the coach's whiteboard due to their online behavior?

Social listening has made the job of recruiting a little easier for those with access to social listening tools.

With social media, character and behavior count more than ever.

To all parents, grandparents, and students out there, learn to be a crocodile... Not a dinosaur. Learn to change and manage the technology and culture before the technology and culture change you and your children.

Failure to manage your online privacy might leave you with, "A lot of 'splaining to do."

16.10 The Internet of Things (IoT)

A few years ago, I first heard of the Internet of Things, or what is more commonly referred to as IoT. Essentially, the Internet of Things is the connection of electronic devices, in homes, cars, and buildings that allows them to be controlled remotely and exchange and compare data.

Such devices could be as simple as the NEST thermostat in your home, a sensor in your car, a medical device that controls your heart rhythm, the lights in your home, a camera on your front porch, or any number of devices that can connect to a network.

What we call SmartHomes essentially allow everything in your home to talk to each other. This technology can help you save hundreds if not thousands of dollars per year on utility costs by being able to automate and remotely control every device in your home.

Projections suggest that at the time of this book's publishing in 2019-2020, there will be 24 billion such connected devices throughout the globe. However, since this is a "green field" industry, it can also create privacy issues.

In the next few years, more cars will be connected to the Internet, allowing them direct communication with SmartCity infrastructure. This might permit the redirection of vehicles during heavy traffic.

Doctors will be able to monitor ailing patients from their homes, reducing the need for inpatient observation and thus reducing healthcare costs.

There are thousands of changes coming to our world due to the billions of tiny sensors embedded in everything from toasters, refrigerators, lights, traffic systems, dams, electric plants and any other aspect of infrastructure that can better serve humanity through an Internet connection.

However, like all progress, there are potential issues, the biggest of which is the impact on our privacy.

A few years ago, when wireless routers that provide Wi-Fi in our nation's homes were first released, the majority of families never changed the security settings of the router. As such, it was easy to drive down your neighborhood street and use your neighbor's Wi-Fi. Moreover, it made it easy to gain access to the devices in their homes. To a lesser extent, that still occurs today.

Now imagine having five, ten, twenty, 100 devices each with their own ID. Without proper security, it will become somewhat easy to hack your neighbor's lights, TV, thermostat and any device that is not properly secured. As the IoT becomes more ingrained in society, product developers realize the need to create easy-to-manage devices and controllers. However, this is still a nascent industry and not every manufacturer of such devices is there yet.

You might be asking, "What value is there to hacking my connected devices?" The answer is, your activity on these devices is part of your private profile.

For example, you watch TV. There might be TV programs that you view that you wouldn't want your boss, neighbors or church clergy to know. Well, a group of researchers from the University of Michigan showed just how easy it is to hack a Samsung SmartThings smart home system. Such hacking could easily provide such TV viewing information in addition to allowing eavesdropping through the connected TV's microphone and camera.

In the case of your car, imagine your driving profile including speed, location, miles driven, accelerations and hard stops being reported to your insurance company. This is already possible today through OnStar and other services. Yet you are making that conscious decision when you register for the service and subsequently request a discount from your insurer. However, would you want private detectives to have such info? What about an attorney in divorce cases?

Could they gain access to your driving information in child custody cases to prove that you endanger your children?

And what about your grandfather's pacemaker? Can that be hacked? The answer is anything can be hacked given enough time, resources and knowledge. This is not to say the IoT should not move forward. It is to suggest that we didn't see the unintended consequences of the smartphone. We should learn from that mistake before we decide to connect our homes, lives, and families to the Internet.

SEVENTEEN

Self Esteem, Stalking & Divorce

I n our most recent survey of teens, we discovered that around 40% of teen girls used filters before posting an image of themselves. In fact, many suggested they might take five to ten photos for Instagram before selecting one that is "just right."

Was this how young ladies really felt? Were they drawn to this app like moths to a flame, with many a similar outcome?

A May 2017 study by researcher Matt Keracher for the UK's Royal Society for Public Health seems to suggest that, "Yes, this is how young women feel about Instagram and why they must carefully curate their image."

"Instagram draws young women to "compare themselves against unrealistic, largely curated, filtered and Photoshopped versions of reality,"

"Instagram easily makes girls and women feel as if their bodies aren't good enough as people add filters and edit their pictures in order for them to look 'perfect,' " an anonymous female respondent said in the report."

In fact, of the top social media apps used by teens in the study, only

YouTube was deemed to have a positive impact. However, YouTube has its own set of issues.

So, let's go back to the year 2007. Steve Jobs is about to walk onto a black, spotlighted stage to reveal his latest, greatest product. As he approaches center stage wearing his black turtleneck, blue jeans, gym shoes, and John Lennon glasses, the crowd await his introduction with nervous anticipation. Everyone in the audience thinks that he'll be introducing several products. However, instead, he surprises most by introducing just one product that has the features and functionality of many. That product, of course, was the iPhone.

I wasn't there, but I recall watching the playback on the web. I was as excited as anyone in the crowd. I had followed Steve Jobs while I was a writer for NCR Corporation. He and Bill Gates were the tech rock stars of my era. But as enthused as I was about the iPhone, I never in a million years would have thought this singular device would play a role in how young women and some young men would perceive themselves.

I would have not thought that this device would become a major vehicle for the growth of bullying and teen depression.

Nor did I think that lives would end on the streets and expressways of our country due to texting and driving.

Although the iPhone was not the first smartphone, it was the first smartphone for the consumer. It caught the public's fancy with little thought to the consequences. Within just a few years, those first iPhones and later Google Android devices would make their way from the hands of parents to those of their children.

As I mentioned in an earlier chapter, our Digital Tattoo series was developed due to the unfortunate suicide of an eighteen-year-old woman. But even I, someone that had researched social media so thoroughly, had little knowledge of how profane the use of social media would grow with teens in our society until one day while visiting a small Catholic grade school about ten years ago in 2009.

The building was located on a quaint, urban campus that appeared to have weathered well the advance of time over its eighty-some years of existence.

The school was run by an articulate, energetic, elderly nun who greeted me with a hardy handshake and bright smile. As with any presentation, I asked her if there had been recent issues of which I should be aware. She paused and then told me that over the summer, a 7th-grade female student I'll call "Jane" had created a fake Facebook account in the name of another female student named "Lori", with the intent to humiliate her. Jane uploaded naked photos and videos that were of another similar-looking female that could be construed to be Lori. Since Lori didn't have social media, she wasn't aware of the fake Facebook account until she returned to school.

She was consequently humiliated by the page and subsequent comments made to her in school when she returned from summer vacation.

Lori's parents and the Principal became aware of the site through comments made by other parents at the start of school. They quickly called the police who in turn felt the Facebook page to be vile enough to contact the county prosecutor.

After reviewing the issue, the prosecutor requested a subpoena from a judge so they could legally secure the IP address from Facebook of the computer that had generated the original Facebook account. In time, law enforcement was able to track down Jane, who had created the original fake account. She was summarily expelled from school and potentially faced both criminal and civil consequences for her actions.

I learned so much in those first ten minutes of my conversation with that elderly nun, not about technology but about the psychology and motivation of young people. She had spent her entire life working with young people. She knew kids over multiple generations. Nothing really surprised her. At the ripe old age of about seventy-five, she had learned the "ins and outs" of children, technology, and the legal system. I was amazed.

Since that time, it appeared that issues related to teens creating fake social media accounts had all but vanished from the ether of "The Network." However, this past year, incidents of such behavior appear to be again on the rise. This time, the app of choice is Instagram.

It begs the question, when is it a crime? Perhaps more importantly, what steps can you take if it happens to you or your child?

17.1 When is it a Crime?

This is not an easy question to answer. What might seem obvious is not always the case. The law is evolving and being interpreted in the light of technology we could never have conceived ten to twenty years ago. In short, it's generally assumed to be illegal to ever provide another person's personal information with the intent to do them physical or emotional harm. But the motivation of one's actions is not always easy to prove.

Some possible illegal scenarios we often see with teens include:

- Stalking and/or posting embarrassing or false information about an individual
- Harassing someone using digital media, websites, apps, etc.
- Logging into another person's social media account without their specific permission
- Threatening another person or using intimidation — including the threat to post something online if they don't provide something to you. This often takes the form known as "sextortion."

Are these actions always a crime? Not necessarily. Remember, each case is different. How each jurisdiction handles such cases will often differ as well. However, I recommend you visit Rise & Stand.

They are a non-profit organization that helps individuals and organizations dealing with such issues. Again, bullying, harassment, identity theft, extortion, and sextortion are all serious issues. Check with the proper authorities in your area before attempting to pursue legal recourse for someone's online actions against your child.

In reality, illegally using social media comes in various flavors. However, the following scenario is somewhat typical of what you might find in middle and high schools.

Scenario:

Jill has been best friends with Julie since the first grade. They vacationed together and have played soccer together for years. However, recently, Jill has become annoyed because of the attention a boy they both like being given to Julie. Since then, they stopped sitting together at lunch and seldom talk in the hallways of their school.

The tension continued to build over the course of a month until Jill decided to get even with Julie by creating a fake Instagram page using Julie's identity. She copied several photos from Julie's real Instagram accounts and from images she screen-grabbed through Snapchat. She then posted them onto the new public Instagram page created as Julie. She also found some inappropriate photos by doing a Google image search and posted them onto the same fake page, alluding that the girl in the inappropriate photos was Julie.

She then sent out friend requests to all of Julie's friends. Many of them were surprised to have received the invites because they were already followers of Julie. However, most went ahead and accepted.

Julie's friends were shocked by the images, with many deciding to shun their long-time friend. However, a few quickly brought the issue to Julie's attention.

Julie was devastated by the Instagram page and the subsequent bullying that ensued by some of the boys and girls in her class. She told her parents of the issue who then immediately contacted the school principal. The principal contacted the school resource officer for his opinion. Given the naked images that appeared on the page and the references to sexual behavior of a minor, the school resource officer contacted the local county prosecutor.

Upon reviewing the same information, the county prosecutor requested that a judge issue a subpoena to Instagram to reveal the IP address of the person that created the fake Instagram account under Julie's name. The judge agreed.

Since Instagram has an entire department responsible for responding to such subpoenas, Instagram turned over the records related to Julie's fake page, including the IP address of the tablet used to create the account. Law enforcement contacted Jill and her parents and eventually revealed all the evidence related to the date, time and IP address used to create the page.

Jill now has a problem:

- There is verifiable proof that her tablet was used to create this fake page. It was the same tablet used to create all of her personal social media pages. Moreover, her parents know she has been annoyed with Julie for the past thirty days and certainly had the motive to attempt to hurt her.
- Since Jill had broken the "Responsible Use of Technology Pledge" in the school's Handbook, the school suspended Jill from class for one week.
- Julie's parents are furious. Their daughter hasn't slept well since the page was created. She has endured hurtful text messages from her classmates and faced embarrassing comments in the halls of the school. Her parents are seeking a civil suit if the criminal courts don't punish Jill.
- Lastly, and perhaps the least of Jill's problems relate to her user agreement with Instagram. Jill violated multiple aspects of the Agreement by posting naked pictures, posting copyrighted material from a Google search, and by creating an account without the permission of Julie. Jill has now been suspended by Instagram.

17.2 Reality Check

In an ideal world, this is how most cases would begin to unfold. The culprit would be found and quickly face the consequences of their parents, school, and the courts. However, this is not NCIS New Orleans. Seldom are crimes neatly wrapped up in sixty minutes, with a detective smugly smiling at the camera as the file is placed into the CLOSED CASE drawer.

In the real world, law enforcement must prioritize what cases should consume the time and treasure of their officers.

Sadly, the growth of heroin, other street crimes and now terrorists using social media smother already-strangled police departments and court systems. If no person is severely damaged by the actions of another, people like Julie's parents might be forced to seek other avenues of justice such as a civil suit or talking it out with Jill's parents and the school system.

While the above scenario involves malice on the part of Jill, often cases involving fake identities are simply pranks. However, they're not without their consequences as well. It can be illegal to access or change someone's social media account and/or password without their permission, even as a joke. The issue grows significantly if you use their account to threaten or extort favors. But again, reality suggests not every breached account can or will be fully pursued by law enforcement. Like many things in this new technology-driven world, the law does not always sync-up with reality. Always check with an attorney before pursuing such cases.

In the United States, we have what is known as the Computer Fraud and Abuse Act or CFAA. There are many areas covered in this act but in large part, it makes it illegal to intentionally access a computer without authorization from the proper owner or management of that system. Unfortunately, the law does not explain what "without authorization" actually means.

CFAA is not to be confused with Identity Theft laws in the United States. Yet, these laws and that of CFAA each play a role in what you or your child may or may not do online. You can find more information on these issues at the website of Stay Safe Online.

Their stated mission is *"To educate and empower our global digital society to use the Internet safely and securely."*

That said, often a parent feels compelled to move forward with a lawsuit. For example, in 2012, after her school and police said that they could do nothing about a fake Facebook page and subsequent cyber bullying, a Georgia teen filed a suit against two of her classmates for creating a fake Facebook account in her name. They distorted photos of her, posted a racist video that implied she hated African Americans and suggested she was sexually active and a drug user.

Cases such as this can be traced back as far as 2007 after an adult named Lori Drew created a fake Myspace account with her teen daughter and another girl to assist in bullying thirteen-year-old Megan Meier. Sadly, Megan later took her own life.

Drew was charged and later convicted under the Computer Fraud and Abuse Act for violating Myspace's Terms of Service by creating a fake account.

Unfortunately, the conviction was overturned by a judge.

17.3 Sharing Passwords

Frankly, sharing smartphones and tablets happens every day at schools across the country. Often, teens know each other's passwords for devices and associated accounts such as email and social media. By logging into one another's accounts and sending messages without permission, teens can face charges as well.

This is particularly important to understand should a message be sent that is vulgar, threatening or contains images of a person under the age of eighteen in the state of nudity or partial nudity. But remember, if you pursue this through legal channels, it is not a guarantee you'll win in criminal or civil court.

Another somewhat related story is worth noting.

In 2013, in New York, there was the case of Ian Barber. Allegedly, Mr. Barber posted naked photographs of his girlfriend (now ex-girlfriend) to his Twitter account. He then also sent the illicit pictures to her sister and her place of employment. Many view this as the first "Revenge Porn Case."

Eventually, among other offenses, he was charged with aggravated harassment in the second degree.

Unfortunately for his ex-girlfriend, the judge dismissed all three charges. You can read more about this story in the article published in *The Atlantic,* titled, What The Law Can and Cannot Do About Online Harassment. This story illustrates how difficult it can often be to win such suits in a system whose laws don't always sync with this evolving technology. Although this scenario had nothing to do with sharing passwords, it indicates how sharing anything online can create havoc for once loving couples or friends.

However, as far back as 2011, articles concerning the practice of trusting best friends or those in a relationship have been written. In fact, that same year, Pew Research revealed that 30% of teenagers that regularly used social media shared a password with someone such as a friend, boyfriend or girlfriend. Girls were almost twice as likely as boys to share.

17.4 Catfishing

No, we're not talking about Hillbilly Handfishing, the reality television show about the noble sport of fishing using only your bare hands and feet. In this case, Catfishing is related to the creation and use of fake online profiles. The reference started as a kind of Internet dating hoax made popular by the 2010 documentary film and MTV reality series. Generally, the motivation for catfishing is for the purpose of developing a misleading internet liaison.

Online teens and adults might simply create a fake profile with seductive pictures or comments meant to lure in their victims. Oftentimes, the victims are individuals with low self-esteem, lonely or simply curious. But that is not always the case.

In fact, the University of Michigan hired the company, 180 Communications to help teach their football players a lesson in how they could be easily lured. The company used a beautiful young employee to send a friend request to every member of the football team. Many were all too eager to oblige.

Beautiful young girl… Athletic young men playing for a high-profile university… What could go wrong?

Fortunately, nothing went wrong since the university was using this as a lesson for their players, i.e., "Don't trust that the person on the other side of the app is who they say that they are."

Don't believe me? Just ask Manti Teo.

17.5 The Role of Schools

All schools throughout the United States and in most Western countries consider cyber-bullying and catfishing to be a serious crime. Most schools have policies against such actions, whether on the school premises or otherwise. At the start of the year, most of these institutions review this policy with their students, often requiring the parents of the student to sign the policy or handbook.

Social media has placed a heavy burden on schools to police the actions taken outside of the school. Social media often creates disruptions inside the walls and on the grounds of the school. To that end, the punishment a school provides might be swifter than that of the court system.

For example, students who bully other students—and in some cases bully teachers—can face suspension or expulsion. Moreover, as we mentioned, the school system might also request the opinion of the local police to determine if a crime has been committed.

17.6 What can you do to protect your child?

Below are five quick steps to consider in protecting your family against having social media accounts breached or children being bullied.

1. Always monitor your own online activity and that of your family:

If you believe that your account—or the account of your child—has been hacked, change your password immediately. Also, most sites have a contact link that allows you to report such suspicious activity.

2. Don't post too much personal information:

Don't post your location, birthday, full name, address, phone number or email address. That makes it too easy to create a fake profile of your information. It also makes it easy for someone to attempt to secure credit in your name and create other social media accounts in your name.

3. Google your name and/or nickname for any fake profiles that might exist about you or your child:

Should you find such a profile, contact the owner of the app or website. If you're a teen, tell a parent, teacher, or school resource officer.

4. Make your passwords strong and don't share:

Use strong passwords and change them often. Don't share the password with friends.

5. Be careful when using free Wi-Fi or public computers:

First and foremost, always sign out of your accounts when finished. If you're using a public computer and don't sign out, others can access your password and information. Also, when using Wi-Fi, it might be easy to record your keystrokes or even access your account if a user on that same network is using the right software.

Too Late! It Happened to My Child. What Can I Do Now?

Most legal authorities will suggest the following steps to anyone who has had their information hijacked. However, we'll also offer you some more pragmatic suggestions at the end of this chapter:

1. Record the evidence:

   This includes screen grabs. Also print any posts that have been directed at or about you.

2. Talk to your teacher, coach, school counselor or principal:

   Most schools in the US and in other western countries have "responsible use of technology" policies that cover cyber bullying and identity theft. If the person involved in such activity attends the same school as the victim, the school may provide more options than the legal authorities. However, ultimately, you'll want to contact the police if the issue can't be resolved through the school. See my next point.

3. Report it to the police:

   If you believe you are the victim of one of the crimes explained above, you should report it to the police. However, if your situation involves a nude or sexual image of a young person, you might want to consider obtaining legal advice before going to the police. Each state varies as to the proper process.

4. If you know the person who created the fake account, ask them to delete it:

   If an account has been created for you, chances are you know who created the account. If they don't represent a physical threat to you, ask them to delete it. If they refuse to delete it, contact a trusted adult, parent, teacher or school resource officer.

5. Apply for a protection order:

Every so often, these issues involve a potentially dangerous person. If this is the case, and you're being stalked, intimidated or threatened, consider applying for a court protection order. In some states, this might be known as a restraining order.

6. Report the abuse to the app or website owner:

It's important that any fake profile created in your name—or any act of cyber bullying—be reported to the app or website owner. For example, if a page has been created in your name, service providers such as Facebook, Instagram and many others have a process you should follow.

————

In the United States, one of the more recognized organizations that helps families and businesses with extortion is FraudSupport.org, a leader in the area of protecting families and businesses against fraud and extortion.

The bulleted points below are from FraudSupport.com and should also be helpful:

•Stop all communication with the abuser or scammer; it's important to not respond.

•Block the abuser or scammer from your phone, email, and/or social media accounts.

•Collect all relevant documentation related to the scam and keep them in a secure file. You may need to provide this documentation when you file a report. Use these Documentation Tips for Survivors of Technology Abuse & Stalking.

•Find out if your local law enforcement agency will take a report at the non-emergency number.

•Report the abuse to the online platform where the scam took place, and if you have wired money or made a payment and suspect it is a scam, contact your financial institution and/or the money service you used right away.

In addition to all of the above, know that stalking and harassment are compulsive behaviors. As such, official warnings and restraining orders may be of little impact, especially over time.

I do not say this to frighten you but so you can take action toward better protecting your child after there has been harassment or stalking behavior. When a perpetrator—child or adult—with a compulsion is 'banned' from going near or contacting a victim, they will feel aggrieved and vengeful, as well as somewhat bereft; the target of their attention has been cut off.

Know that in many cases, legal recourse may be of limited effect, especially as the frustration builds in the offender over time.

In the light of the above, take the following additional measures if possible:

- Ensure the child goes nowhere unaccompanied, ideally by an adult;

-Give the child an attack alarm and show them how to use it;

-Consider the child carrying a personal tracker. Many apps work well but a dedicated tracker is less likely to be found by a perpetrator, who'd look for the child's phone first of all. Trackers do not necessarily look identifiable and can be hidden well within clothing or in a bag.

Tracker devices show second-by-second movements that are accurate to a pinpoint, and many come with inbuilt alarms. Your child can have a tracker working all year round for under $300 including charges.

It is surprising how many kids will agree to a tracker being carried quite voluntarily! It is also fun when they have the chance to accrue months of data about where they were every second of a day!

-Tell everyone who knows the child that there is a problem. Agree an emergency plan with friends and relatives;

-Discuss whether your child will agree to a monitoring app being installed on their phone. This will show all incoming and outgoing communications and may help you spot a problem your child would not see;

-Above all, talk to your child openly about the problem, how they feel, and that you are taking it seriously. Even if they seem to brush it off, knowing you are still taking care of the issue is a silent reassurance.

17.7 When everything else has failed

If you've received no relief from law enforcement or your school, there are steps you can take to possibly find the individual who created a fake social media account in your name. To do so, you may wish to consider subscribing to a service such as Spokeo.com.

Every new social media account requires an email address at the point of registration. They also require that you provide a different email address in the event they need to contact you.

Since email services such as Gmail and Yahoo are so easy to create, offenders often quickly create a new email account using one of these two services. These email addresses are generally linked to an email account they actually use.

If you know the email address associated with the fake social media account that is in your name, Spokeo can often find other emails created by the person who used that address to create that account. There are many such people search websites that aggregate data from online and offline sources. However, these sites have at times been very controversial and require a monthly fee.

For example: If a student named John Doe created a fake Instagram account related to James Johnson, he would have likely used another email account to do so. To that end, if he created an email account named jamesjohnson#1977@gmail.com — Google makes him use an existing email account that can be used in the event Google needs to contact him.

Spokeo searches all email names that have been used to create such accounts. If John Doe does not have his privacy settings set to friends only, there is a good chance his real email and name will be displayed during the Spokeo search.

If you think you know who created the fake social media account, and you have a name, phone number or email address for the person, Spokeo will also find most email addresses and social media accounts created by that person. If your fake page was created by the individual under suspicion, there is a chance it will appear during your Spokeo search.

Unfortunately, no approach is guaranteed to work every time. However, if it does, James Johnson now has the person's name that created the fake account and perhaps many others. At that point, James' parents can contact John Doe's parents, school or the police.

EIGHTEEN

The Wild, Wild West

W e are very much living in the era of the wild, wild West when it comes to policing digital ne'er-do-wells. Technology that was created to help bring society together often is used to break it apart. In schools, the petty jealousies and popular cliques of the past continue today but are emboldened due to the scope, power and, at times, the perception that social media is anonymous.

The greatest means of protecting your family's online communication is to keep the lines of communication open at home. Children know what is going on at their school and with their friends. They often know when other children are having problems with classmates in the school or online. Knowledge and subsequent action are key to circumventing problems.

Make certain your children understand some of the points we've addressed in this chapter. However, understand that with the constant evolution of apps, it takes vigilance to keep ahead of those that might not have your best interest at heart.

As the wise elderly nun taught me, you're never too old to learn.

18.1 The Big Green Brain

In 1899, while Samuel Clemens, aka, Mark Twain was living in Sweden, he wrote an article that was eventually published in Harper's Monthly Magazine about fifteen years later. In his essay, Clemens waxed poetically about the use of pictures as memory devices. Given his many tours on the speaker's circuit, Clemens often used images in place of notes when he delivered his speeches.

> Clemens said, "...*you can tear up your pictures as soon as you have made them—they will stay fresh and strong in your memory in the order and sequence in which you scratched them down.*"

Given his success with this method, he felt these "tricks" would help children absorb the lessons of history.

I spend many hours each week heeding his advice, attempting to find just the right image or video to help students better understand the good, the bad and the ugly consequences of social media.

A few years ago, I was looking for such images when I came upon an animated video of a transparent head with a green brain floating and slowly rotating through the ethers of the universe. I was captivated by its outwardly omnipresent form which seemed to possess the ability to see, know and tell all, while having no empathy for its victims.

I needed that big green brain to tell the story. The story of how digital devices and the corresponding apps potentially see everything that you do, record everything that you do, and potentially distribute everything that you do. So, with the help of $25, I purchased the digital rights to the big green brain and set out to tell the story.

Perhaps no better example of the big green brain's power was exhibited by Curt Schilling, the former baseball great that put the hurt on two "virtual thugs" who had hidden behind pseudonyms as they trash-talked Schilling's daughter with rude, misogynistic rants on Twitter.

The trash-talking Twitter tantrums were in response to Schilling's proud post congratulating his daughter Gabby's acceptance to college where she'd be playing softball. The post was met with a flurry of mean-spirited, highly sexualized and somewhat violent comments directed at Gabby.

Like any self-respecting father, Mr. Schilling's protective shield was raised as he vowed to "out" the craven provocateurs, lashing back and revealing their real names, jobs, and colleges they were attending. I'm sure each was shocked by how quick, accurate and overwhelming Mr. Schilling's reply was.

One of the miscreants known on Twitter as "The Sports Guru" was a DJ at Brookdale Community College in New Jersey. He has since been suspended by the school for violating its standard of conduct.

Another virtual assailant purportedly was the VP of the Theta Xi fraternity at Montclair State University and a ticket-seller for the Yankees. Upon learning the identity of the individual, he was subsequently fired by the Yankees. These situations are great illustrations of the power of the big green brain.

18.2 Did Curt Schilling Create Bigger Issues?

While most fathers, myself included, would stop at nothing to protect our children, I'm not certain Mr. Schilling didn't create more problems given his response. He now has raised the ire of every self-loathing cretin on the Internet by his "shock and awe" offensive. This only garnered more hate-filled responses on social media that followed him and his family.

Additionally, given his public profile, telling the world where his daughter will be attending college is also an invitation for problems. If the "creepy guy down the street" didn't know about Mr. Schilling's daughter beforehand—he does now.

18.3 Take 10

If social media were not a major part of my career, I might have reacted in much the same way as Mr. Schilling. However, the last slide in our live presentations to teens perhaps provides the best advice for

everyone young and old when considering a social media comment…
"Take 10."

Before ever sending a tweet, posting a Snap or responding to
another user, take ten seconds, ten minutes or ten hours and think
about the consequences of your actions. I'm sure The Sports Guru, the
VP of the Theta Xi fraternity at Montclair State University and even
Curt Schilling wish they had taken that same advice before they
entered 140 characters to elicit laughter or seek revenge.

18.4 Social Media & Lost Careers

In the 2016 article in People Magazine, 20 Tales of Employees Who
Were Fired Because of Social Media Posts, courtesy of Reddit, writer
Lydia Price mentioned several cases where employees lost jobs due to
inadvisable social media posts.

Of the twenty listed, these three were my favorites:

*"A prospective employee at the company I work for had just passed his
interview and was told that all he needs to do is pass a drug test and a physical
and he would start on Monday. Someone found the new hire on Facebook and
the guy had just posted 20 minutes after the interview, 'S—! Anyone know
how to pass a drug test in twenty-four hours?!'"*

*"I had to fire an employee for a tweet he wrote about a customer. He tweeted
'(customer's full name) would be a great name for a porn star.' I found out
about it when the customer's lawyer called me the next day threatening action.
Turns out the guy worked for the local newspaper and obsessively searched his
name on all social media."*

*"A girl I know was a nurse at a hospital and got fired for posting things on
Facebook such as: 'Soooooo sleepy here in the ICU. Will someone please code
and give me something exciting to do? #isthatbad?' and a lot of racist things.
The dumbest part about it was she was TAGGING the hospital she worked at
in her posts."*

18.4 Privacy, Divorce & Social Media

Recently, a study published in the Journal of Cyberpsychology, Behavior and Social Networking, determined that the frequency with which Facebook users log into their accounts can create a "Facebook–related conflict" with their better half.

Such conflicts often lead to breakups or divorce. The scientific study was conducted by Russell Clayton, at the University Of Missouri School Of Journalism in conjunction with a team at the University of Hawaii at Hilo and St. Mary's University in San Antonio. Collectively, they surveyed 205 Facebook users between the ages of eighteen and eighty-two.

79% of these users suggested they were in the midst of a romantic relationship.

The study's hypothesis was that one's overly frequent social media use and the monitoring of a partner could lead to relationship issues.

The study suggests a correlation between the use of Facebook and the steadiness of the romantic relationship. One might further assume the same is true for all social media.

You don't need to be a psychologist to understand that the more time spent focused glaring at a glowing screen means less time to have a conversation with your partner. Moreover, as other studies have shown, many folks have reconnected with former romantic interests via social media. This was much more difficult prior to the rise of social media.

In a 2015 article in the Huffington Post, entitled New Survey Says, Stay Off Social Media (Or Risk Divorce), Brittany Wong wrote:

> "...Divorce attorneys agree that social media has increasingly played a part in marriage breakdowns. In 2010, 81% of divorce attorneys surveyed by the American Academy of Matrimonial Lawyers said they'd seen an increase in the number of cases using social networking evidence in the five years prior. The attorneys said Facebook was the number one source for finding online evidence, with 66% admitting they'd found evidence by combing the site."

It probably didn't take a survey to determine these results.

However, it helps to prove the point. There is limited time per day. The time you spend on social media is the time you can't spend with your partner or child.

18.5 Data, Data, Data

Today, data from government, marketing companies, and social media are easily aggregated and bought and sold. It's often easy to determine the real names of so called "alias cowboys" by simply knowing just one identifying piece of information, such as their pseudonym, email address, home address or other information.

As I mentioned earlier, services such as US SEARCH, Intelius, and others aggregate databases from auditors' sites, court records, social media sites and other publications, often with incredible accuracy. The cloak of darkness for most such offenders is often quickly eliminated—particularly by people with the financial means such as Schilling. However, most of these services cost less than $10.00 per month and often will surprise you by the richness of information they have on almost everyone. But as I mentioned earlier, they have been very controversial and don't always provide the value that their monthly fee requires.

Privacy does not exist.

NINETEEN

Video Games

O ften during my social media presentations for adults, at least one parent asks about certain video games. In 2018 and the start of 2019, the question generally involved Fortnite, the hit video game produced by Epic Games. In the unlikely event you've not heard of Fortnite, I'll give you a quick overview. But first let's address what is happening in the area of video games.

Based on trends over the last few years, first-person shooter video games have become quite popular. First-person shooter games or (FPS) are video game genres centered around weapon-based combat from the perspective of a first-person. In other words, you experience the action through the eyes of the central character.

These games have also become spectator sports. Just as people are willing to watch grown men run through tacklers or hit a tiny ball off a tee, today's digital gamers are growing fans by the thousands. I encourage you to look at the pages of Twitch, the epicenter of video gaming. They are filled with digital stars with names like Myth, Mtashed, and LuLuLuvely. Millions follow such stars and there is sponsorship money for them through companies such as Gillette, Intel and others. I'll address Twitch momentarily.

But understand, in the world of social media and video gaming, things change. The keeper of monitoring such change is AppAnnie. According to their stats from July 9th, 2019, Fortnite had dropped to number seven on the list of video gaming gross revenue, just behind Clash of Clans, Roblox, Golf Clash, Toon Blast, Candy Crush – and coming in at number one: Dragon Ball.

Never heard of most of them?

If you have a child who plays video games – you should have.

At its height, Fortnite was growing in popularity among both young men and young women, as was its competition called Players Unknown's Battlegrounds, better known as PUBG, and Apex Legends.

Like many games, Fortnite has a dystopian theme – in this case set in contemporary Earth where a destructive storm causes 98% of the world's population to disappear. Zombie-like characters rise to attack the remainder, which would include you if you're playing the game.

As many as four players can work together on missions which involve randomly generated maps. Your objective is to fight the storm and protect survivors, while building weapons to engage in combat.

The adoption of Fortnite seemed to come out of nowhere as word travelled by word of mouth on school buses, in lunchrooms and study halls by teens across the globe. In a February 26th 2018 article by Mack Ashworth, he suggested the most recent high total of concurrent users on Fortnite was 3.4 million.PUBG's high was 3.2 million. So, it's close to a toss-up on user count between the two.However, during the period of March 2018 through April of that year AppAnnie showed Fortnite was number one or two in video games downloads throughout the period.

19.1 Is Fortnite Violent?

Yes… but in a cartoony kind of way. Unlike other games such as Call of Duty or Grand Theft Auto, these charters are far less real – thus there is not the blood and guts we've grown accustomed to in other games.

19.2 Should parents be concerned about violent video games?

The American Psychological Association said this in their July 2016 guideline on media violence in video games:

"There is convergence of research findings across multiple methods and multiple samples with multiple types of measurements demonstrating the association between violent video game use and both increases in aggressive behavior, aggressive affect, aggressive cognitions and decreases in prosocial behavior, empathy, and moral engagement."

However, in a CNN interview, a contrary view was cited by Dr. Whitney DeCamp, Associate Professor of Sociology at Western Michigan University, who suggested that the evidence points to either no relationship between playing video games and violent behavior or an "insignificant" link between the two.

Decamp said, "Basically, by keeping young males busy with things they like, you keep them off the streets and out of trouble."What's my perspective? I'll give you my ice-cream analogy. You wouldn't let your kid eat ice-cream daily for ten years. You know it's not good for them. However, every child that does will not necessarily develop Type 2 Diabetes, although some will.

As adults, we know it's not good to eat that much ice cream. But a little is not so bad. However, there are individuals who are genetically predisposed to get type 2 diabetes if they don't monitor their sugar intake.

Similarly, in our digital world, we need to manage our kids' digital diet. As parents, we need to better manage what games kids are playing but more importantly how long are they playing, and with whom. We need to be parents. Some children might be environmentally or genetically predisposed to acting out violently by their exposure to violent video games and through excess hours spent playing them.

19.3 Are Fortnite and other first-person shooter games destroying schools?

Probably not… but there certainly is a concern. There's not a school at which I have spoken where a teacher hasn't mentioned the issue concerning the amount of time students dedicate to this game.But Fortnite, PUGB, Apex Legends and others are less important than where such games can be played.

The fastest-growing content and technologies being adopted by teens are video game live streaming platforms such as Twitch and its competitors, YouTube Gaming, Mixer and Caffeine.

What? You've never heard of Twitch, YouTube Gaming, Mixer or Caffeine? Well… most working parents haven't either, but if you have a child that you've allowed to do online video gaming, you should. This area of teen interest is moving faster than the adoption rate of social media after the release of smartphones in 2007 and 2008.

The granddaddy of them all, Twitch, has continued to grow over the years, and is almost the unchallenged leader in this space. Due to this popularity, they are attracting the competitors I mentioned earlier.

One word of caution: if you're offended by foul language or sexual innuendo, tread softly on the Twitch site or similar recordings on YouTube. Both live and recorded video feeds can be rated R or worse.

Why is there so much interest in this space? Money.

There is money to made by Twitch and its competitors, but there is also money to be made by the gamers and content creators.

The reality, what I call "gaming hubs", are turning into entertainment networks. They will eclipse network TV and some streaming services. In ten years, the major TV networks will not exist in their current form.

In the case of the newest competitor, Facebook Live's online gaming, one gamer already has over 1 million followers. Whether it's Twitch or the other competitors, they each have their own unique monetization models for sharing ad revenue. Some of these players and content developers are getting rich.

Let's just focus on Twitch for the moment.

If you understand Twitch, you'll understand the attraction and the competition. Twitch is a live-streaming video platform owned by

Twitch Interactive, a subsidiary of Amazon.[3] It's both an app and a website. Launched in 2011, it focuses on video game live streaming including broadcasts of eSports competitions, in addition to music broadcasts, creative content, and more recently, "in real life" streams. Content on the site can be viewed either live or via video on demand.

By 2014, it was considered the fourth largest source of peak Internet traffic in the United States. By May 2019, Twitch had 15 million daily active users, with one million of the users being online at the same time.

So why have 99.9% of parents never heard of Twitch?

I don't have that answer, but if you have a child that plays online videogames you must know what I call the "Twitch Neighborhood" And it's NOT Mr. Roger's Neighborhood.

If you have given a device to a child and you don't know anything about the technology, the youth culture and the apps and website they visit, that's akin to giving the keys to your Porsche to your twelve-year-old and telling them to get home by 4:00am. You wouldn't do it. And you can't do it with technology. But parents do this all the time.

Although watching others play a video game on Twitch seems rather tame, the language and bullying often is not. As such, Twitch recently released a profanity and bullying filter, and many have called for better policing of the sexual content.

For example, the famous—or should we say infamous—girls of Twitch are often video gamers as well, but many of them make money by dressing proactively and doing things on camera for their audience. Although not actually pornography, they at times go right up to the line, and sometimes cross it.

Newer features on Twitch called "cheers" are animated emojis that viewers or fans purchase as tips sent as chat messages. These are actually very similar to functions on web chat platforms. Additionally, some actually charge viewers to be followers.

19.4 Twitch & Banned Content

On the plus side, Twitch users are not allowed to stream any game that rated "Adults Only" (AO) in the United States by the Entertainment Software Rating Board.

Twitch has also explicitly banned specific games from streaming, regardless of rating. However, it has NOT banned games such as Mortal Kombat X, Grand Theft Auto or The Witcher 3. Should your thirteen-year-old be playing or watching these games be played?

Twitch has tried to help charities with special online events and are now streaming some professional sports and a lot of eSports. Obviously, Twitch is not all bad nor is it all good. But if you've never been there, you can't make that decision.

As parents, we need to look at social media as a part of a large city. Within that city are neighborhoods. Like all neighborhoods, there are a few homes you don't want your kids getting near because of the unsavory characters that live in those homes.

If you think that way, you'll better understand that kids don't differentiate between the real world and the virtual world.

You can't either.

Twitch is a neighborhood in a very large digital city. So are Instagram, Snapchat, Tik Tok and others. There are some homes in that neighborhood that contain people and activities that could adversely influence your kids. If you know those homes and people, you can help your kids navigate the app or website.

If you can't, perhaps you need to reconsider why you gave your child the ability to access them in the first place. Video games are apps that require time spent in digital neighborhoods.

They are generally interactive and will influence your child in one way or the other. You need to know the neighborhood and activity just as you do in the real world.

TWENTY

Date Rape, Teen Boys & Porn

On December 7th of 2018, three men gathered in a house in York County South Carolina. Such a gathering would not be considered unusual, particularly during a time when the holidays are approaching. On December 8th when none of the men returned home, family members went to check on their well-being. Sadly, they found all three had passed away. There were no marks on their bodies or signs of violence. Authorities believe the carbon monoxide from a heater or grill was the cause of their demise.

On December 9th, 350 miles away in the Midwest, a young man was in the home of an eighteen-year-old woman that he knew. A few hours later, he was arrested on rape and sodomy charges.

The young lady with whom he visited had visible signs of physical abuse over several parts of her body. Today, this scenario is often called date rape.

On the surface, these two events seem to have nothing in common. Yet they very well might share the fate of unintended consequences.

The burning of coal and wood and other means of keeping warm were developed for the betterment of mankind. However, it would take years before humans understood that if used in un-vented areas, there would be deadly consequences due to a silent killer.

Based on years of experience, we know that carbon monoxide–sometimes known as "the silent killer"—is the most common type of fatal air poisoning in many countries today.

It is colorless, odorless, and tasteless, but deadly. It is the unintended consequence of burning wood to stay warm.

But what about the story of the young man charged with rape or sodomy? While we don't know of his innocence or guilt, we are beginning to understand why a young man with a promising life would possibly violently rape a young lady he had known. Was this a case of an unintended consequence?

You'll see what I mean momentarily.

20.1 Boys & Porn

A new study conducted at the University of Nebraska, determined that based on the age of first exposure, a man's attitude toward women is "negatively shaped from the first time he is exposed to pornography."

In other words, the age of the first encounter with pornography significantly impacts the view of women and sex in the eyes of the man or boy.

The group surveyed 330 undergraduate men between the ages of seventeen and fifty-four. 85% of those participating in the survey were white, with 93% of those being heterosexual.

Each participant was asked the following questions:

- At what age did you first watch pornography?
- Was it accidental, intentional or forced?

They were then asked forty-six additional questions to determine if they fitted two masculine norms:

- Playboy (promiscuous)
- Seeking power over women.

As I stated earlier, their findings suggest men who had watched porn at the earliest ages would behave more aggressively and dominant toward women.

Men watching porn later in life would more likely engage in promiscuous behavior but not necessarily act violently toward them.

In Peggy Ornstein's book, Girls & Sex, she states that while researching her topic she spoke with more than seventy young women between the ages of fifteen and twenty concerning their attitudes and early experiences with types of physical intimacy.

During her interview on NPR's Fresh Airs with Terry Gross, she said, "pop culture and pornography sexualize young women by creating undue pressure to look and act sexy. These pressures affect both the sexual expectations that girls put on themselves and the expectations boys project onto them."

Having read her book and heard the girls' varied experiences with sex and the "bro" culture, it would appear her observations are correct if not downright depressing.

In fact, last month I was speaking to a group of psychologists about teens' use of technology. One told me that he is seeing a significant change in the sexual expectations of young men toward the women they are dating. He feels that the sex boys see in porn becomes an expectation when they begin to date. This expectation is supported in Peggy Ornstein's book.

Well you might be thinking, that's all very well and good, but what is the unintended consequence?

I'm getting there...

20.2 This Changes Everything

On January 9th, 2007 as he was about to introduce the iPhone, Steve Jobs stood on a stage in San Francisco and told 4000 reporters and industry analysts, "occasionally, a revolutionary product comes along that changes everything."

Jobs was right. The introduction of the iPhone has largely changed not just life in America, but nearly everywhere and everyone. For the most part it's been positive, but like all advances in technology, it introduced its share of problems and unintended consequences.

Jobs never envisioned a world where kids as young as eight to nine years of age would have access to an iPhone. Yet the average age a child gets a smartphone in America is ten, trending toward nine. The average age a child first sees porn is aged eleven. Coincident?

Which brings me to the very serious topic and unintended consequence related to date rape—and why that early access to porn mentioned above might well be a factor.

20.3 We Gave Them the Keys

By 2011, adults that had purchased iPhones and later Android phones began updating their devices. Often, they would hand down those devices to their children without understanding that those devices connected their kids to the world and the world to their kids.

For example: 56% of children, aged eight to twelve have a cellphone.

Today, a child viewing porn is almost mainstream.

The non-profit Childline Abuse Registry in Pennsylvania has voiced its concerns. To illustrate their apprehension, one boy under the age of fifteen told ChildLine that he was "always watching porn, and some of it is quite aggressive. I didn't think it was affecting me at first, but I've started to view girls a bit differently recently and it's making me worried."

To be honest, for every study you find on the pitfalls of pornography, you will find another study suggesting that viewing porn is not an issue. However, we have only had about ten years to understand how instant access to porn might impact teens.

In years past, pornography was limited to print on glossy paper. By the 1990s, porn video cassettes were popular, but not easy to play on your parents' VHS deck. Porn "addiction" was unlikely if you could only view it the few times Mom and Dad went on a date.

Today, we have the first generation that can watch porn seven days per week, twenty-four hours a day at any time and any place.

Porn today is professionally produced, with almost broadcast-quality lighting and 1080 HD resolution. In fact, Virtual Reality Porn is viewed in 3D with 180-degree vision of the scene. The viewer is part of the action using VR goggles.

We are in the midst of an unintended experiment on a whole generation.

Baby Boomers remember the drug, Thalidomide that was first marketed in 1957 in West Germany. Unknowingly, this wonder drug was prescribed as a sedative or hypnotic. Thalidomide also claimed to cure, insomnia, gastritis, and tension. It was a miracle!

However, before long, between 5,000 and 7,000 infants were born with malformations of the limbs. Fewer than 50% of these children survived.

The drug later made its way to America and had similar repercussions. A generation was impacted by the 'unintended consequence' of a drug.

20.4 Is today's mobile porn the Thalidomide of the past?

We don't know if the young man in the Midwest is guilty as charged. But if he is guilty of date rape, is it due in part to the young man's opinion of women that he adopted from viewing porn at a young age? I don't know.

But pornography, much like carbon monoxide, has silently invaded our homes and now the very devices we have given our children. Highly sexualized images of women entered our TV sets during prime time while we were lulled into a false sense of security with Hollywood censors.

It could very well be the Thalidomide of the 1950s has resurfaced as a digital drug under the auspices of porn, "malforming" the brains of many young men and, in the process, the lives of young women.

When all is said and done, victims of date rape don't care why it happened; they simply want to heal.

As a society, we must take steps to understand why this happens and make certain it doesn't happen again. Frankly, I'm not confident this will occur.

The solution starts when we pay attention to the access we've given our kids to the world, and the access that the world has to our kids.

TWENTY-ONE

Social Media & Teen Mental Health

We have likely all seen this situation before. You go to your favorite fast food restaurant to buy a cup of coffee or burger, and the employee behind the POS terminal is a young teen boy or girl. They take your order, and while giving you your change, you notice scars on their arms. Were they burned by the deep fryer? No. Most likely they participated in the ugly trend of cutting.

Having been married to a teacher for over forty years, I am keenly aware of the issue where teens use self-harm as a coping mechanism. Somehow, the cutting of the skin and subsequent bleeding brings a sense of relief to the problems of their lives. Sadly, I see this all too often in my travels to area schools. In fact, speak to any guidance counselor in a middle school, and they can likely tell you story upon story of teens and tweens that have sought such relief.

Anxiety concerning divorce, grades, and relationships, abuse in the home, financial hardships, sexual identity, bullying and any other problem can bring on such actions. Many children hide these marks from their parents, choosing parts of their body that go unseen by Mom and Dad.

In an August 15th, 2019 article in the Wall Street Journal, by

Mary Pipher and Sara Pipher Gilliam, they interviewed 100 girls between the ages of twelve and nineteen to better understand how young women feel about living in this digital world.

One young lady named Genevieve, aged sixteen, said,

"Honestly, sometimes I wish we were living in the 'olden' days, when kids hung out with friends and went on dates."

Young Americans that are now part of the ADT have become unwitting guinea pigs in today's huge, unplanned experiment with social media, and teenage girls like Jordan are bearing much of the brunt. In conversation after conversation, adolescent girls describe themselves as particularly vulnerable to the banes of our increasingly digital culture, with many of them struggling to manage the constant connectedness of social media, their rising levels of anxiety, and the intense emotions always central to adolescence.

Many in the mental health field believe that self-harm is on the rise, and perhaps is one of the most troubling symptoms of a wider psychological problem plaguing 21st-century adolescents.

Teen depression and anxiety have been escalating since 2012 after several years of stability. It's an occurrence without demographic bounds. As I have seen in my own travels, it cuts across the inner-city, through suburban towns and rural townships. It doesn't care if you're white, black, Asian, Hispanic, gay, transgender, straight, rich or poor.

According to a 2015 study by the Department of Health and Human Services, about 3 million teens between the ages of twelve to seventeen have had at least one major depressive episode in the past year. Additionally, at least 2 million reported experiencing depression that hurt their ability to function on a daily basis.

Perhaps even more perplexing, according to data from the National Institute of Mental Health, approximately 6.3 million teens have had an anxiety disorder.

In a May 2017 study in Translational Psychiatry, researchers found that:

"Projecting from age-specific incidence proportions, the cumulative incidence

of depression between the ages of 12 and 17 is 13.6% among male and 36.1% among female subjects. The sex difference in incidence is significant at the age of 12 years."

To put teen mental health concerns into even closer perspective, consider these stats from Cincinnati Children's Hospital:

The number of youth mental-health assessments in Cincinnati Children's emergency department rose from 4,362 in the fiscal year 2011 to 7,864 by mid-2017. This equals a 10% increase, year over year. Moreover, as we mentioned in an earlier chapter, Cincinnati Children's Hospital has seen a 70% increase of children treated for anxiety and depression between 2011 and 2015.

Additionally, in the Greater Cincinnati area which has a population of about 2.2 million people, there were sixteen known adolescent suicides between January and June of 2017. Certainly, not a record anyone hopes is broken.

Rachel Ehmke of Child Mind Institute, writes in her article How Using Social Media Impacts Teenagers:

"Peer acceptance is a big thing for adolescents, and many of them care about their image as much as a politician running for office, and to them, it can feel as serious. Add to that the fact that kids today are getting actual polling data on how much people like them or their appearance via things like "likes." It's enough to turn anyone's head. Who wouldn't want to make herself look cooler if she can? So kids can spend hours pruning their online identities, trying to project an idealized image. Teenage girls sort through hundreds of photos, agonizing over which ones to post online. Boys compete for attention by trying to out-gross one other, pushing the envelope as much as they can in the already disinhibited atmosphere online. Kids gang up on each other."

In our 2016 survey of nearly 10,000 students between the ages of twelve and nineteen, about 18% of respondents said they had been bullied online. Over 20% stated they had suffered through depression. Many of the students felt that such online negativity toward each other led to their depression. By 2019, over 30% of teens said they had been bullied.

Some of their unedited comments shed light on teens' online lives:

- *They text a lot and also sometimes will spread rumors about people. Also, at one time, there was an Instagram account called DMS Crushes that could spread rumors or private information.*
- *People are making accounts about students and not revealing who they are.*
- *People are constantly on social media, always posting. Also, people who post rude things about other people.*
- *I've heard that a person took a vid of their sister naked and showed it to someone.*
- *The new trend is creating "spam" accounts where teenagers make their profile private and only let certain friends follow them. They post funny, rude, and personal things that they wouldn't like the rest of the school/world to see. What they don't know is that their profiles are not as private as they think.*
- *Here's what sucks. It's that no matter what you do, people will still find a way around it. People still won't care and disregard everything said to them. This generation is disgusting. Everybody is offended by everything and other people just trying to live normal lives are affected by them, and their over-protective parents who couldn't dare to imagine their kid's stupid third-world gender that doesn't even exist. No matter what anybody does, this problem will not be fixed. Ever. It's been around since the beginning of time. So until people learn to stand up for themselves, and take control of themselves, nothing will get better. Social media is just the feeling place, and quite frankly, just the beginning of something great and horrible.*
- *People become fake when they get on social media as they change their personality to fit society's image of how they should be.*
- *People send mass nudes images. I could receive like twenty in one day if I wanted.*
- *They are very rude and don't consider people's feelings at all.*
- *Some people use it to blackmail people with pictures.*
- *Unfortunately, yes, even at my age nudes are sent. But it's really*

hard to be shielded from everything inappropriate online, so just trust that most of us will be responsible.

- *No, I don't bully people online. I get bullied online.*
- *Some kids post embarrassing photos of other people or even their friends, that hurt their feelings.*
- *People get into fights 24/7 on Social Media sites.*

In some respects, these are the same petty issues as years past. However, there are trends today that take place both in and out of school hours, twenty-four hours per day. This constant barrage of teen commentary and comparison makes teen life more difficult, particularly when you consider they often have no physical or time boundaries.

As we have found in our own discussions with school counselors, depression and anxiety are often under-reported by the teens themselves. Although most children would willingly report a broken leg, fever or stomach issues, there continues to be a stigma attached to mental health issues. Therefore, healthcare professionals often can't help until the problem becomes obvious. At that point, it could be too late.

In fact, according to a 2015 report from the Child Mind Institute, it was determined that only about 20% of young people with a diagnosable anxiety disorder get treatment.

In her October 27th, 2016 article in Time Magazine, Teen Depression, and Anxiety: Why the Kids Are Not Alright, writer Susanna Schrobsdorff said:

"In my dozens of conversations with teens, parents, clinicians and school counselors across the country, there was a pervasive sense that being a teenager today is a draining full-time job that includes doing schoolwork, managing a social-media identity and fretting about career, climate change, sexism, racism—you name it. Every fight or slight is documented online for hours or days after the incident. It's exhausting."

And yet we have given digital devices to our kids and in many cases exacerbated the problems. We've not provided or demanded technology-free zones. Kids have unfettered access to everyone seven days per week, 365 days per year. Conversely, the world has access to them as well.

Teens are often comparing their lives, their bodies, their accomplishments to those of their peers or even the celebrities that they admire.

Additionally, as parents, we are often physically present but mentally absent from their lives as we glare at the glowing screen in our own hands, comparing our family, our home, our boat, our car, our kids, our spouses to those of the many friends and acquaintances in our "friends" lists. Although we wonder if our kids listen to us, I can tell you they do observe us.

21.1 Empathy & Narcissism

Narcissism is a growing concern among mental health care providers throughout our country. Social media and poor parenting are sometimes defined as the main culprits in building teenagers that are self-centered and insecure.

However, by nature, teens are self-centered and insecure. Most children are still trying to understand life and create real assessments about themselves while developing judgment skills. They also feel impervious to life's consequences.

In reality, there is generally never one reason for the growth of any one disease, societal ill or cultural trend. However, there is no denying there is a growing lack of empathy among teens and their peers.

Patricia J. Manney, an American writer and speaker, posted an Op Ed in the June 2015 edition of Live Science. In her post titled, Is Technology Destroying Empathy? she wrote:

> "I had explored empathy creation since 2008 when I published a paper entitled "Empathy in the Time of Technology: How Storytelling is the Key to Empathy" in the Journal of Evolution and Technology. Empathy works on a neurological system that scientists are still trying to understand, involving a "theory of mind network" that includes emulation and learning. But at the center of empathy creation is communication.

.... But for all that information and exposure to new ideas, there are many examples of communication technologies that can destroy empathy. Let's begin with the ideological information silos of broadcast, print, website and social media, where conservatives or liberals only listen, read and watch their own thoughts repeated in recursive echo chambers of increasingly radical and exclusionary thought."

Having visited nearly 400 schools over the past ten years, I have seen how teens and adults tend to get their information from a few select sources. They often share concepts and articles from these sources and consequently have a limited view of the world and each other. There are seldom opposing views allowed. And when such views are voiced, they are sometimes shouted down, or the opposing individual is bullied.

We, of course, see this in adult life via cable TV news. For example, each news network, admittedly or not, has its own perspective on what is news. If we only follow one news source—which often happens—we have a limited view of the world. Our patience for and knowledge of opposing views become limited.

We grow angry and assume the worst of many from the other side. We lose our empathy.

This trend has created division within our country. It ultimately demonizes or dehumanizes the opposing point of view. It's very easy to see when observing political debate. It's everywhere, seven days a week, twenty-four hours per day.

Now take this theory and apply it to teen life.

Imagine what you see on TV where democrats and republicans scrutinize every word, turn of a phrase, choice of tie or haircut, and then transition that concept to your child's social group.

Particularly for girls, their completion, body type, make-up, jewelry, shoes, and clothes are under constant scrutiny. They repetitively track their likes on Instagram as if it validates them as humans. Not enough likes? Take down the post and do a better job of curating your photos in the future.

As adults, we understand what I call "spin media."

Not everything we see and hear is true. Children often can't discern what they see and hear—and sometimes don't hear—within their peer group.

If a child is facing other stressors in their life and they feel their peer group is defaming them or ignoring them, it can be the proverbial straw that breaks the camel's back.

As we know, children grow physically in their early teen years. But what is unseen is the mental growth that takes place. For example, face-to-face interaction is vital to learning how to read and express emotion. However, 60% of the synapses in the brain disappear if they aren't used between birth and adolescence. Since the national daily average for teens being online is nearly seven hours a day, one might assume that their emotional IQ will be negatively impacted.

Not all is bad. There is evidence that social media can offer our children positive emotional benefits. For example, Teens can and do often connect with their peers more easily through social media and texting and messaging apps. As such, they often feel supported through their network of *positive* online friends. The key word is "positive" online friends.

With these networks and online stories, they can be exposed to information and other's life experiences they might not have otherwise witnessed. This can be very positive—or at times negative.

21.2 Depression & Suicide

In a recent study by the International Center for Media & the Public Affairs (ICMPA) study:

> *"Students around the world reported that being tethered to digital technology 24/7 is not just a habit, it is essential to the way they construct and manage their friendships and social lives."*

It's easy to read news accounts of social media gone bad and determine that no child should have access to this "heathen devil' technology. Social media and technology are often used for more good purposes than bad. Yet we can't overlook the inherent dangers that exist when it is misused.

Sadly, part of my job takes me to places I'd rather not be. I'd rather not hear the painful social media stories that children often share with me. I'd rather not hear the stories that parents share concerning their child's addiction to online pornography.

I'd rather not hear stories concerning a child being hospitalized due to suicide ideation or a child being buried due to death by suicide.

I'd rather not hear about a thirteen-year-old's depression due to a naked photo she sent to her boyfriend being shared at the school.

Yet this is why this book is written, to cast light on a subject so often swept under the carpet of our society.

That amazes me, with new studies showing how the increased use of apps such as Facebook and Instagram correlates with low self-esteem and decreased life satisfaction. We now know that the constant over stimulation created by social networking can turn the nervous system into fight-or-flight mode, which makes teen depression and anxiety worse.

This problem is amplified when we consider that 76% of teens use social media, and 50% of teens feel they are addicted to their mobile devices.

By June 2017 in Greater Cincinnati, fifteen teens and an eight-year-old took their own lives. It was an unprecedented number in this beautiful river city. This trend is exhibited throughout the US. In fact, one of the wealthiest areas in the United States has one of the highest teen suicide rates in the country.

According to a 2017 CDC Report in the March 3rd Mercury News, during the period 2003 to 2015, Palo Alto's youth suicide rate per 100,000 people was 14.1. The national average is 5.4.

Epidemiologic Assistance (Epi-Aid) studies performed by the CDC address urgent public health problems ranging from outbreaks of infectious diseases, to the effects of natural disasters and deaths by suicide.

According to the CDC, such reports that focus on death by suicide include:

- Capturing trends in fatal and nonfatal suicidal behaviors in

youths, including the number of deaths, visits to emergency
rooms and hospital discharges
- Examination of whether print media coverage of suicides
  meet guidelines suggested by mental health professionals
- Inventory and comparison of local youth suicide prevention
  programs; policies related to national recommendations; and
  making recommendations on strategies for the school,
  community and county levels.

In the Palo Alto case, researchers reviewed 246 articles that
addressed suicide deaths and determined that media outlets did not
follow proper suicide reporting guidelines. Such guidelines caution
against sharing too much detail related to the method of suicide,
photographs of memorials or grieving relatives and friends. This is all
part of what is called the contagion theory.

There is a theory that too much focus on suicide and even the
romanticizing of death by suicide can create a contagious response by
others. In fact, in the case of the death of suicide of Jessica Logan, she
had just attended a funeral of a friend who died at his own hands. She
returned home and took her own life.

21.3 Live Streaming Suicide

In her July 6, 2017, article in Philly.com, entitled, Livestream suicides:
Does it influence our kids, Terri Erbacher, Ph.D., Clinical Associate
Professor, Philadelphia College of Osteopathic Medicine wrote:

"Now, with the advent of Facebook Live, social media is another avenue for our
youth to unexpectedly view violence. Since it began in 2015, more than more
than 45 acts of violence—including suicide—have been live streamed for the
world to see.

Livestream suicides greatly increase the number of persons exposed, which
increases the possibility of contagion—the phenomenon through which
exposure to suicide can lead to another's suicide attempt. This is particularly
troublesome among adolescents who may already be struggling, and perhaps
contemplating suicide."

The contagion effect has been studied since the 1990s by the Center for Disease Control. In their paper, the CDC reported:

"One risk factor that has emerged from this research is suicide "contagion," a process by which exposure to the suicide or suicidal behavior of one or more persons influences others to commit or attempt suicide. Evidence suggests that the effect of contagion is not confined to suicides occurring in discrete geographic areas. In particular, nonfictional newspaper and television coverage of suicide has been associated with a statistically significant excess of suicides. The effect of contagion appears to be strongest among adolescents, and several well publicized "clusters" among young persons have occurred.

"These findings have induced efforts on the part of many suicide- prevention specialists, public health practitioners, and researchers to curtail the reporting of suicide – especially youth suicide – in newspapers and on television. Such efforts were often counterproductive, and news articles about suicides were written without the valuable input of well-informed suicide-prevention specialists and others in the community."

Today, news media generally do a better job of being sensitive to how they report suicides. Yet, at times we still see news programs depicting mourning families and friends, impromptu memorials, and interviews with those that knew the victim. Although we can't hide reality from our kids, we, as a society, need to make certain we are not sensationalizing or glorifying such acts. To a child struggling with their own internal issues, it can create additional trauma.

21.4 Thirteen Reasons Why

Then there is the concern over the original Netflix TV series, Thirteen Reasons Why. According to the Netflix program information:

"Katherine Langford plays the role of Hannah, a young woman who takes her own life. Two weeks after her tragic death, a classmate named Clay finds a mysterious box on his porch. Inside the box are recordings made by Hannah – on whom Clay had a crush – in which she explains the thirteen reasons why

she chose to commit suicide. If Clay decides to listen to the recordings, he will find out if and how he made a list. This intricate and heart-wrenching tale is told through Clay and Hannah's dual narratives."

Although the program is well done and sheds a bright light on an issue plaguing our nation, there is concern among mental health care providers that the program might only add to the problem.

Recently, there had been a series of teens take their lives using live broadcast apps. Shobhit Negi, a Psychiatrist in Howard County, Maryland, shed some light on the issue in the Baltimore Sun article Teens Turn to Social Media for Attention, Even in Death.

"Posting to the world the deliberate act of ending one's life can possibly serve different purposes. The combination of the quasi-feeling of connectedness instilled by social media and the feeling that one can control one's actions in the privacy of the bedroom or bathroom might take away the solitary feeling of the suicide act. The combined weight of vulnerability, need for validation and limited decision-making capacity might make it difficult for some youth to step back once they have posted something pertaining to suicide on social media."

To my knowledge, in the past five years, I have known only a few students who went on to take their lives. However, I have heard many stories from teens about how they or their relatives have been hospitalized, or in some cases taken their life.

The first situation involved a twelve-year-old girl whose mom approached me at a presentation. Her daughter, who I'll call Monica, had become a victim of identity theft when another student created a fake Instagram page in her name and then populated the page with pornography of a girl performing sex acts.

Monica, her mom, and Monica's best friend asked me to help find the person who posted the images and the fake account. I referred them to the police chief that was standing no more than ten feet from me. However, I gave the mother my card and asked her to contact me if the police chief couldn't help.

About two weeks later, I got a call from the mother. She wanted to tell me that Monica had suffered significantly over the past two weeks.

The embarrassment and humiliation were difficult for a twelve-year-old mind to manage. She then went on to tell me that they found the person responsible for the posting. To my surprise, the offender was Monica's best friend.

Apparently, Monica was receiving attention from boys at the school. Monica's friend was jealous of the attention and decided the humiliate Monica.

In another case, a young man approached me following a presentation to a group of high school students at a small, Catholic high school. The boy thanked me for the presentation and then told me, "You're right." I asked him what he meant by his comment.

He went on to tell me his cousin had taken his own life when someone created a fake Instagram page and populated it with homosexual pornography. He told me that the police attempted to track down the offender but had no luck.

Knowing the digital footprint such actions almost always leave behind, I contacted the local prosecutor about the case. However, when we dug a little deeper, we discovered that indeed the culprit had been found—in Europe.

How the young man that had taken his life was humiliated by someone in Europe is still unknown. Yet, as I point out in my presentations, it's difficult to escape the metadata—or digital tattoo—left behind during any online communication.

There are countless other stories I could share about my experiences. Most of them today tend to blend in with one another. So many times, the stories are the same.

Only the student and school generally differ. However, almost always there is an element of anxiety and depression that either result from the experience – or the experience is due to the depression, anxiety or lack of self-esteem.

21.5 What Parents Can Do

First, we must watch the warning signs, quickly determining when help is necessary and getting our child a professional assessment and treatment. Again, remember, teen depression and anxiety have been on the rise for over ten years. There has been much research that suggests teens displaying symptoms of depression and/or anxiety are not getting the proper treatment.

As we will detail in our last chapter, the parent must place parameters on a child's online time, their access to certain apps and the places where they may use technology. Bedrooms and bathrooms should be off-limits. This is where many intimate conversations take place. Often these conversations lead to actions that will further a child's stress.

We as parents must continue to speak with our kids, not to them. Understand why your child wants to use technology and certain apps. Communication with your child is the key to good parenting.

Also, be certain your child subscribes to the rule of good living: Body, Mind, and Spirit. Life is about balance and is the pillar of success. How they sleep, what they eat, and their outdoor activity is just as important as the grades they get in school.

We will go into greater detail about managing and monitoring your child's online activity in our final chapter.

21.6 Online Gaming & Griefing

For the past 20 years, I have taught Catholic CCD and PSR classes at my parish to 6th graders each Tuesday evening. My first year of teaching was 1997. That year, the video game business was growing with such platforms and Nintendo 64 and PS1.

For those of you of a certain age, you might recall the release of the Palm Pilot that year as well. Every self-respecting businessperson in the IT industry was ditching their Franklin calendars for a Palm or other PDA device.

A few years later, in April of 2000, the first Blackberry Smartphone made its way to the market, usurping the Palm Pilots, Trios and HandSpring devices of that era.

However, for the kids in my class, they seemed to be unaffected by the change in technology. Few of their parents had Blackberry Smartphones or PDAs.

However, I noticed a shift by 2010 as more families purchased iPhones and later iPods, DSi's and other Wi-Fi enabled platforms. It was at this time the first student approached me about being bullied online by a 35-year-old man.

Wi-Fi has brought incredible benefits to our world. However, it also has brought to your child's door pedophiles and bullies under the auspices of competitive game play. These actions are often called "griefing" or "trolling."

Gamepedia.com defines griefing as:

"Griefing is the act of irritating and angering people in video games through the use of destruction, construction, or social engineering. Popularized in Minecraft by teams, griefing has become a serious problem for server administrators who wish to foster building and protect builders. Most players tend to dislike and frown upon griefing, while others feel it adds a certain degree of drama to the game. Trolling, while most thought very similar to grieving, is not always known as the same thing. Griefing is normally malicious, while "trolling" is usually used in more of a joking manner."

Whether one's actions are meant to destroy, anger or to joke, such activity can play havoc with a teen already under stress in other areas of their life.

In his March 2017 article, Bullying's newest frontier: Rise of gaming's online abuse and 'griefing,' Alastair Roberts defined griefing in even more detail.

"Online abuse in gaming or 'griefing' has become a popular form of entertainment for some gamers. If you search 'griefing' in YouTube, you will come across thousands of videos that advertise themselves with "...made them cry" or "...kid cries," these videos often involve adults or teens purposefully targeting young users within the game and intentionally acting in a way to anger or upset the player."

Certainly, the anonymous nature of online gaming and internet communication makes many of us bolder. However, the growing lack of empathy we mentioned earlier likely plays another role in this trend.

21.7 Pedophiles and Gaming

The issue of pedophiles is another great concern for parents whose children are using such online games.

In a January 2019 Newsweek article by Katherine Hignett, she details how a man named Anthony Gene Thomas, 41, of Broward County, used *Fortnite* to find and groom his victim. This ultimately led to the man engaging in sexual activity with the minor while also requesting graphic images and videos. According to Florida's Attorney General, there could be up to twenty other victims.

In April of 2017, a mother of an eight-year-old boy told the NBC affiliate in New York City that her son was "groomed" by a sexual predator on the popular Roblox game. Roblox has over 50 million monthly users and allows each player to chat with other users. Sadly, this is how the boy was apparently targeted.

According to the mother, the predator portrayed himself as another child and would often partner with him while playing the game against others. However, the discussions escalated to personal questions and requests for photographs.

Google "pedophiles and video gaming," and you'll read countless similar stories, many ending more ruthlessly than in this example.

21.8 Mental Health Help

Each time I present to teens, I walk that tightrope of defining real-world consequences for kids that misuse technology. I try to make certain kids know that their lives are not over if they experience digital persecution from peers, or if they make a mistake online. Life can go on.

As parents, teachers, clergy, and mentors, we must understand that we are blessed to have many resources to help teens and their families deal with this brave new world. Beyond A Wired Family, there are many websites, apps and books to help. One resource to help better understand cyber bullying is the Cyberbullying Research Center. This site can help you better understand social media's place in self-esteem development.

If you feel your child is being harassed online, intervention programs can certainly help both you and your child. Consider visiting the National Suicide Prevention Lifeline or the Substance Abuse and Mental Health Services Administration's (SAMHSA) What a Difference a Friend Makes website.

Remember, social media is NOT the only cause of depression, anxiety, and suicide ideation. However, we would be naïve to think the growth of such issues is not somehow a significant contributing factor. By understanding the trends of technology and how your child uses social media, you stand a better chance of protecting your child from the temptations and dangers of this evolving world.

However, not to be overlooked is the role a child's faith plays in overcoming mental health issues and adversity. We'll look at that in our next chapter.

TWENTY-TWO

The Role of Faith

D uring the entire period of the Vietnam War, over 58,000 US soldiers died. By any measure, that number is almost unimaginable. However, last year, almost 45,000 people in the United States took their own lives. That is a 25% increase over 20 years.

Spending on mental health in the United States more than doubled during that same period but has had little or no impact. Moreover, among adolescents, the incidence of at least one major depressive episode per year has risen by over 60% during the past decade to reach 13.3%. However, some studies have shown depression among girls to be as high as 36%.

In the May, 2017 publication of Translation Psychology titled: Sex differences in recent first-onset depression in an epidemiological sample of adolescents, the findings are most disturbing. Below are two quotes from within the paper's abstract.

"Data from six consecutive years (2009-2014) of a national survey of US adolescents aged twelve to seventeen are used to characterize sex differences in the incidence of depression by age and to compare recent first-onset and

persistent depression with respect to impairment, suicide attempts, conduct problems and academic functioning. Projecting from age-specific incidence proportions, the cumulative incidence of depression between the ages of twelve and seventeen is 13.6% among male and 36.1% among female subjects."

"... The incidence of depression during adolescence is higher than that suggested by prior studies based on retrospective recall. Contrary to prior studies, evidence suggests that the sex difference in depression originates during childhood and grows in magnitude during adolescence. High levels of impairment, suicide attempts, conduct problems and poor academic functioning argue against a 'wait and see' approach to clinical treatment of recent first-onset depression."

As we find teen depression and suicide increasing over the past decade, there is some positive news. There is significant evidence suggesting increased religiosity may be *associated* with better mental health. For research purposes, the term is defined as how often individuals pray or attend religious services. Additionally, it relates to the importance an individual places on his/or her religion.

In a survey conducted by Jane Cooley Fruehwirth in conjunction with Sriya Iyer, an expert on the economics of religion at the University of Cambridge, and Anwen Zhang, an economist at the University of Glasgow, the team investigated a unique dataset, the National Longitudinal Survey of Adolescent to Adult Health. The team focused on high school students including questions on depression, and religiosity.

Religiosity decreased the probability of being at risk of moderate to severe depression by 11%. Ironically, the most compelling results were that the effects were almost two-thirds greater for the individuals with the most severe symptoms of depression. As Jane Cooley Fruehwirth said:

"This finding offers a startling contrast to evidence on the effectiveness of cognitive-based therapy, one of the most recommended forms of treatment, which is generally less effective for the most depressed individuals, at least in the short term."

The study also found that religiosity could help reduce stressors such as a decline in physical health or the loss of a loved one to suicide.

Perhaps even more interesting is that their research finds that teens with fewer support structures at home or in school experience more benefit through religiosity.

Similarly, Pew Research in their January 31, 2019 article, *Religion's Relationship to Happiness, Civic Engagement and Health Around the World* found that those with a relationship to their faith were happier than those who had no faith or did not practice their religion.

The article states, "This analysis finds that in the US and many other countries around the world, *regular participation in a religious community* clearly is linked with higher levels of happiness and civic engagement (specifically, voting in elections and joining community groups or other voluntary organizations). This may suggest that societies with declining levels of religious engagement, like the US, could be at risk for declines in personal and societal well-being. But the analysis finds comparatively little evidence that religious *affiliation*, by itself, is associated with a greater likelihood of personal happiness or civic involvement."

In the U.S., religion tied to some measures of health, happiness and civic engagement

% of U.S. adults who say they _____ among those who are religiously ...

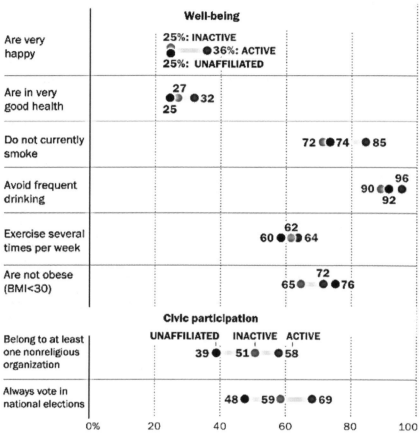

Well-being

Are very happy
- 25%: INACTIVE
- 36%: ACTIVE
- 25%: UNAFFILIATED

Are in very good health
- 27
- 25
- 32

Do not currently smoke
- 72 ●74 ●85

Avoid frequent drinking
- 96
- 90 ●●
- 92

Exercise several times per week
- 62
- 60 ●●64

Are not obese (BMI<30)
- 72
- 65● ●●76

Civic participation

Belong to at least one nonreligious organization
UNAFFILIATED   INACTIVE   ACTIVE
- 39● 51● ●58

Always vote in national elections
- 48● 59● ●69

0%   20   40   60   80   100

Note: Frequent drinking is defined as drinking several times per week. The actively religious are those who identify with a religion and attend religious services at least once per month. Inactives are those who identify with a religion and attend less often. Unaffiliated are those who do not identify with a religious group.
Sources: Happiness data for United States from Pew Research Center's 2012 Gender and Generations survey. Data on drinking, smoking, obesity and exercise come from the International Social Survey Programme's 2011 Health and Health Care module. Data on civic engagement and health come from 2010-2014 World Values Surveys.
"Religion's Relationship to Happiness, Civic Engagement and Health Around the World"

PEW RESEARCH CENTER

In another Pew Research titled, *Diversity, Gender Equality, Family Life and the Importance of Religion,* Jacob Poushter, Janell Fetterole and Christine Tamir focused on four subjects:

- Is diversity on the rise?
- Has gender equality increased?
- Does religion play a more or less important role than in the past?
- Are family ties stronger or weaker than they used to be?

Prevailing view is that diversity and gender equality have increased, while ties to family and religion have faded

% who say over the past 20 years ...

				No change
Our country has become **more diverse**	69%	10% Less diverse		16%
Gender equality has **increased in our country**	68	8 Decreased		22
Religion has a **more important** role in our country	27	37 Less important		22
Family ties have **strengthened** in our country	15	58 Weakened		22

Note: Percentages are medians across 27 countries.
Source: Spring 2018 Global Attitudes Survey. Q7, Q9, Q11 & Q13.
PEW RESEARCH CENTER

These Pew Research results were indeed disappointing:

- Roughly six in ten across the countries surveyed say that family ties have weakened.
- A median of 37% say religion plays a less important role in their countries than it did twenty years ago, while 27% say it plays a more important role.

In our A Wired Family survey with 2500 students in Ohio, Indiana and Kentucky, we found that students seemed to be both close to their parents and their faith as compared to the national survey. However, keep in mind, our questions were posed differently than those of Pew Research.

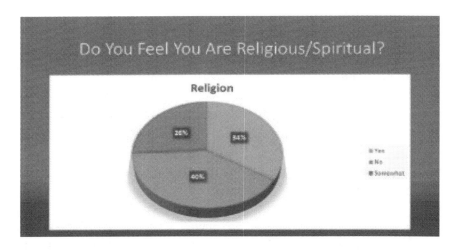

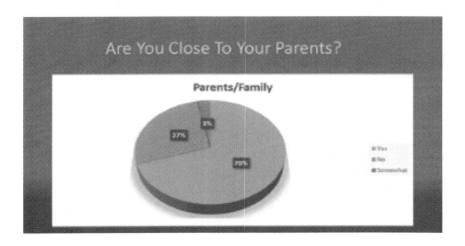

TWENTY-THREE

Managing Your Child's Online Activity

For the past few years, we have presented the "four-prong strategy" to better managing your child's online activity. In 2017, in our Simon Says Take Ten Steps Forward article, we recommended ten steps, but with the advancements in smartphone capabilities and new parental controls, we have reduced the total to four simple actions.

1) Talk to your child and your peers

When working with your child, it's essential to set expectations related to appropriate and inappropriate uses of technology. Understand that if your child is at least twelve years old, there is an excellent likelihood their friends' parents have already provided technology to their children. Moreover, your child's friends are already using YouTube, Instagram, Snapchat, Twitter, TikTok, and others. If you choose to allow access for your child to such technology, you'll need to control what apps are allowed on their devices.

This requires that each member of the family has a contract regarding what they may or may not do with their device. Periodically review the contact and make sure everyone is living up to the agreement. You can download our BARK and A Wired Family contract here. Tech Contract for Families and Kids

It's also essential to speak with your peers, other parents and teachers and share your own experiences. Living in an information age without the benefit of conversation—or, viewing life only through your own experiences, is a bit short-sighted. I have learned more from speaking with teachers, counselors, police officers, students, and other parents than I have by simply reading and doing research.

Reach out and start the conversation at your child's school, your neighborhood, and church or recreation center. Share what you know and listen to what others say.

2) Create a Tech-Free Zone

Depending on your child's age, consider creating a tech-free zone. This might include the dinner table, bathroom, and bedroom. Keep in mind that although technology has increased our ability to communicate with people outside of the home, it has sorely damaged our ability to communicate with those most dear to us.

We are not simply suggesting this approach for managing your child's online behavior; it is also suggested for the adults in the family.

In fact, it's reported that one out of five divorces is blamed on Facebook. In the study published by the Journal of Cyberpsychology, Behavior and Social Networking, researchers determined that people who use Facebook excessively are more likely to succumb to marital or relationship issues.

An entire website is devoted to helping people whose relationships have ended due to social media. Limiting where devices may be used will help reduce the temptation for your child to send something they'll later regret. It might also make you think about limiting your own access to technology.

As for your kids, remember they are children whose brains are not fully wired. As such, their decision-making is severely hampered by hormones, incomplete brain development and lack of experience. They need your help to avoid temptation and misuse of technology. They might hate you today but they'll thank you tomorrow.

Are you allowed to take your device into your bedroom overnight?

Device In Room

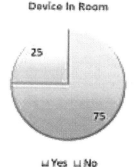

⊔ Yes   ⊔ No

As the stat indicates, 75% of kids are allowed to sleep with their phones. The bedroom is where the majority of sexting takes place. Since 25% of American teens have sent nude pictures, this is a significant reason for minimizing access to devices at night. Moreover, teens sleeping with their phones is a significant cause of teen sleep deprivation.

3) Know Their Account Passwords

If your child is under the age of 16, you and only you should create and know the password to your child's iTunes or Google Play account. As a parent, you should be the only person authorized to download apps to that device. Moreover, once an app is downloaded, there might be another fifteen minutes that would allow your child to download other apps without your knowledge.

As you will see in the video link, you can control when a password is needed and whether a fifteen-minute window for downloading an app is appropriate for your family. We suggest that a password is always required with each download of an app,

We can't emphasize this enough; don't give the device back to your child until you're confident it will require your password for any additional app downloads.

This is important since many apps are available that hide other apps from parents. Often these "stealthy" apps are used to hide photos, text messages and videos from parents and other adults. In our most recent survey, almost 20% of teens are using these ghost or vault apps.

Once this app is on their device, it might be difficult to find. If you haven't been following this approach you should go back over your purchase history on iTunes and GooglePlay to see what apps might have been purchased. You can learn more in the video below.

4) Use Parental Controls

Most parents don't have great confidence in their carrier's parental controls. If you fall into that category, you have several options – each of which is likely better than those provided through your carrier.

There are many on the market that monitor your child's activity, including my favorite, BARK. Although BARK and other controls won't manage your router, it will arm you with a robust dashboard that familiarizes you with your child's activity and warns you of any risky or inappropriate online interactions. The cost is less than $10 per month and is all web-based. As such, there is no software that you need to download to your phone, PC, or tablet.

Photos and videos uploaded to most social media apps such as Instagram, Facebook, Youtube, and others will be viewable by you. However, it will not provide your child's activity on Snapchat, Kik, and WhatsApp. However, you can learn more about the apps supported by Bark in the video below.

Other parental controls can be found in this most recent publication by PC Magazine. Most of the controls listed have strengths and weaknesses. However, more than likely, each parental control company likely paid the publisher for consideration.

TWENTY-FOUR

Conclusion

E ach generation of parents has its own set of obstacles in raising children. However, this is the first generation of parents whose kids potentially have 7/24 access to the world —and similarly, the world having access to their children. As one mom told me following my presentation, "The task of raising kids with this technology is simply daunting." Another parent suggested, "I didn't sign up for this."

These two comments remind me of a funny albeit accurate quote from an unlikely source of parenting expertise, i.e., actor Adam Sandler. "One thing I do know about being a parent, you understand why your father was in a bad mood a lot."

That might be one of the most accurate quotes about parenting that I have heard. Like most parents, I had bad moods each time I was paying bills at the end of the month. To add to my parenting legacy, my kids and loving wife nicknamed me The Mad Muppet due to my frequent eruptions after paying bills for tuition, utilities, pets, mortgages, car payments and the occasional detours the kids made on their journeys through the teen years.

Raising kids is daunting. Technology is daunting. But, if you provided your child a device, you did sign up for this.

My mantra during each presentation has been, "If you don't understand today's technology, you'll never understand and manage what will be here tomorrow."

What is fascinating to me is that parents today grew up during the dawn of the Internet and watched the evolution of technology.

The window to what was coming had been open for years. However, many refused to look. For example, most experts agree that Six Degrees, released in 1997, was the first recognizable social media site. It allowed users to upload their profile and create new friendships with other users. That sounds a bit like Facebook.

In 1999, the first blogging sites came online, and today, versions exist by the millions. Does this sound much like the evolution of what is now called Redditt or Tumblr?

If you're in your mid-30s to mid-40s, you no doubt were exposed to chatrooms and instant messaging platforms. This technology allowed you to stay in contact with friends and family at any time and any place your desktop could plug into an Internet connection. The future for what is now today's technology was written on your dorm wall years ago.

Because we adopted the technology for ourselves as adults, many felt it should be used by children. Perhaps it would bring parent and child closer through better communication.

The smartphones and devices we have provided to our children don't always bring us closer. Often, a child is in the same room with parents but neither is genuinely present if their eyes and nose are staring down at a blue screen.

Smartphones have somewhat diluted a parent's impact on their children as the views of every culture are often front and center each day while their child uses their devices. Questions that in past generations were asked to a parent or caring adult are now the domain of Google and Wikipedia, sometimes leaving the parent's ability to curate answers provided by such sources.

Unlike past generations, kids can update their parents on their location and activities. Unfortunately, when they use this same technology at home, parents often feel less close, less involved, and at times, less of a parent.

This same technology has become every bit the distraction to parents as it has to their children. Oddly, in some households, the most precious gift provided to us by God has become a secondary player to their attention.

In even the safest communities in the Western world, parents lock the doors and set home security systems in fear of a break-in or a fire. But many parents haven't the faintest idea of the actual dangers related to social media or how to guard a child against such threats.

Being a parent in any generation is hard and sometimes ever-evolving. But what has not changed with every generation of parents is the need to be caring and wise. Parenting might be different today than when you were growing up in the 80s and 90s, but your love, wisdom, and attention are every bit as necessary.

If there is one item you take from this book concerning being a parent of a child in this digital world, it would be to talk, to ask questions and listen to your child's response at every opportunity. If you're driving them to school, talk to them.

If you're at the dinner table, talk to them. If you are together in your living room, talk to them. The Adolescent Digital Tribe is talking to them in music, TV, films, social media, billboards, on the street, in the cafeteria, and the classroom. This is their filter bubble.

Your words and actions are just a small portion of what your children ingest each day. But they are the most important of all.

Allow me to leave you a quote from former First Lady, Barbara Bush:

"At the end of your life, you will never regret not having passed one more test, not winning one more verdict or not closing one more deal. You will regret time not spent with a husband, a friend, a child, or a parent."

Good luck with the most critical job you'll have in your lifetime: Being present. Being a parent.

Research References

Foreword

Wall Street Journal
https://www.wsj.com/
articles/SB10001424127887323716304578480883218514720

A Wired Family
www.awiredfamily.org

CNET: A Brief History of Android Phones
https://www.cnet.com/news/a-brief-history-of-android-phones/

eMarketer: Teens Ownership of Smartphones Has Surged
https://www.emarketer.com/Article/Teens-Ownership-of-Smartphones-Has-Surged/1014161

Parents Against Underage Smartphones
http://www.pausamerica.com/

Chapter 2 - The Consequences of Sending Inappropriate Content

Statistic Brain: Sexting & Teens
http://www.statisticbrain.com/sexting-statistics/

Washington Post: Is Sexting the New First Base?
https://www.washingtonpost.com/news/parenting/wp/2014/10/
06/sexting-is-the-new-first-base-yes-maybe-even-your-child/?
utm_term=.60b98758eaf3

US Library of Medicine: Teens Sexting and its Association with Sexual
Behavior
https://www.ncbi.nlm.nih.gov/pmc/articles/PMC3626288/

The New Yorker: The Story of Amanda Todd
http://www.newyorker.com/culture/culture-desk/the-story-
of-amanda-todd

Gloria Allred: Dangers of Teen Sexting
http://criminal.lawyers.com/juvenile-law/gloria-allred-dangers-of-
teen-sexting.html

Definition: Sextortion
https://en.wikipedia.org/wiki/Sextortion

Trend Micro: Sextortion in The Far East
https://www.trendmicro.de/cloud-content/us/pdfs/security-
intelligence/white-papers/wp-sextortion-in-the-far-east.pdf

New York daily News: California Teen Sextortion Plot
http://www.nydailynews.com/news/crime/mastermind-teen-usa-
sextortion-plot-18-months-prison-article-1.1724809

The United States Department of Justice: Man Who Extorted Minors
Produced Child Pornography Is Sentenced

https://www.justice.gov/usao-ndga/pr/man-who-extorted-minors-produce-child-pornography-sentenced

CBC NEWS: Aydin Coban Sentenced in Netherlands for Fraud & Blackmail
http://www.cbc.ca/news/canada/british-columbia/aydin-coban-sentenced-netherlands-online-fraud-blackmail-1.4027359

IMDB: Shut Up and Dance
http://www.imdb.com/title/tt5709230/

CNN MONEY: Sextortion, Thorn Study
http://money.cnn.com/2016/06/23/technology/sextortion-thorn-study/

WEBPRO NEWS: Microsoft, Teen Sextortion Is Common Online
https://www.webpronews.com/microsoft-teen-sextortion-common-online-2016-09/

Chapter 4: A Distracted Society

The Andy Griffith Show
http://www.imdb.com/title/tt0053479/

Highlights Magazine: State of the Kid
https://www.highlights.com/state-of-the-kid

Stephen King: Children of the Corn
https://en.wikipedia.org/wiki/Children_of_the_Corn

Chapter 11: Pornography

Leave It to Beaver
https://en.wikipedia.org/wiki/Leave_It_to_Beaver

Jacobellis v Ohio
https://en.wikipedia.org/wiki/Jacobellis_v._Ohio

Johannes Gutenberg
https://www.biography.com/people/johannes-gutenberg-9323828

French Post Cards
http://www.wondersandmarvels.com/2016/06/the-naked-truth-about-french-postcards.html

Hugh Heffner & Porn
https://www.biography.com/people/hugh-hefner-9333521

Therapy Associates: Teens & Porn
http://therapyassociates.net/

Newsweek: Japan & Virtual Reality Porn
http://www.newsweek.com/vr-porn-samsung-gear-virtual-reality-477369

Navigating Pornographic Addiction
https://awiredfamily.files.wordpress.com/2017/03/3444d-navigatingpornographyaddiction-aguideforparents.pdf

Nine Things You Should Know About Pornography & the Brain
https://www.bellevue.org/9things-pornography

Chapter 13: How and Why Our Privacy is Invaded

Quora: What Is the Meaning Behind the Quote *Plastics* in The Graduate?
https://www.quora.com/What-is-the-meaning-behind-the-quote-plastics-from-The-Graduate

Extractmetadata: Metadata Reader

http://www.extractmetadata.com/

PetaPixel: Lawyer Digs into Instagram's Terms of use
https://petapixel.com/2016/12/07/lawyer-digs-
instagrams-terms-use/

Salon: My Embarrassing Picture Went Viral
http://www.salon.com/2013/
10/02/my_embarrassing_picture_went_viral/

Introduction of the i-Phone
https://en.wikipedia.org/wiki/IPhone_(1st_generation)

Ashley Madison
https://www.ashleymadison.com/

Have I Been Pwned?
https://haveibeenpwned.com/About

Who Is Ricky Ricardo?
https://en.wikipedia.org/wiki/Desi_Arnaz

Fox News: The Case of Darek Kitlinski
http://www.foxnews.com/politics/2015/07/20/key-lawmaker-
demands-answers-from-dea-following-fox-news-report.html

The Letter: Song by Joe Cocker
https://en.wikipedia.org/wiki/The_Letter

What Are Cookies?
https://en.wikipedia.org/wiki/HTTP_cookie

David Patraeus Scandal
https://en.wikipedia.org/wiki/David_Petraeus

New York Times: Hillary Clinton eMail Scandal

https://www.nytimes.com/interactive/2016/05/27/us/politics/
what-we-know-about-hillary-clintons-private-email-server.html

Snapchat's Privacy Agreement
https://www.snap.com/en-US/privacy/privacy-policy/

The History of SmarterChild
https://en.wikipedia.org/wiki/SmarterChild

eMarketer: Messaging Apps Reach 1.4 Billion Users
https://www.emarketer.com/Article/Mobile-Messaging-Reach-14-
Billion-Worldwide-2015/1013215

Venture Beat: Facebook Has 11,000 ChatBots
https://venturebeat.com/2016/06/30/facebook-messenger-now-has-
11000-chatbots-for-you-to-try/

Fight the New Drug: Internet Porn
http://learn.ftnd.org/

Forbes: Kik Porn Bot Spammers
https://www.forbes.com/forbes/welcome/?toURL=https://www.
forbes.com/sites/parmyolson/2014/08/20/kik-porn-bot-
spammers/&refURL=&referrer=#6e85c7046f05

TechJunkie: The Best Kik Bots
https://www.techjunkie.com/best-kik-bots/

Using Spoofed Wi-Fi for Mobile Attacks
https://blog.lookout.com/spoofed-Wi-Fi-60-minutes

Internet Watch Foundation: Where Do Your Inappropriate
Images Go?
https://www.iwf.org.uk/

CNBC: Your SmartPhone Could Be Hacked

https://www.cnbc.com/2016/06/17/your-smartphone-could-be-hacked-without-your-knowledge.html

Gold Frog: Yen VPN Myths Debunked
https://www.goldenfrog.com/blog/myths-about-vpn-logging-and-anonymity

TrickSeek: Free Proxy Servers for School Access
https://www.trickseek.org/free-proxy-sites-list-top-proxy-servers-for-school/

A Wired Family: Parental Controls
https://awiredfamily.org/2016/04/25/managing-your-homes-router-network-beam-me-up-grandma/

Facial Recognition Software
https://en.wikipedia.org/wiki/Facial_recognition_system

The Daily Caller: Facial Recognition Technology Hels NY law Enforcement
http://dailycaller.com/2016/08/29/facial-recognition-technology-helps-ny-law-enforcement-catch-100-identity-thieves/

Tech Target: What Is Machine Learning?
http://whatis.techtarget.com/definition/machine-learning

TechCrunch: Someone Scraped 40,000 Tinder Photographs
https://techcrunch.com/2017/04/28/someone-scraped-40000-tinder-selfies-to-make-a-facial-dataset-for-ai-experiments/

Voactiv: Hacked Tinder Photos
http://www.vocativ.com/425644/hacked-tinder-photos-artificial-intelligence-data-research/

What is Google Vision?
https://cloud.google.com/vision/

What is Amazon Rekognition?
https://aws.amazon.com/rekognition/?sc_channel=PS&
sc_campaign=acquisition_US&sc_publisher=google&sc_medium=
rekognition_nb&sc_content=recognition_exact&sc_detail=facial%
20recognition%20software&sc_category=rekognition&sc_segment=
179121306436&sc_matchtype=e&sc_country=us&s_kwcid=
AL!4422!3!179121306436!e!!g!!facial%20recognition%20software&
ef_id=WQiPTgAAAo1b4_L8:20170503121457:s

Michele Borba, Ed.D BOOK, Unselfie: Why Empathetic Kids Succeed
in an All About Me World
My Book

Indy Star: College Athletes, Your Reputation is Always on the Line
http://www.indystar.com/story/sports/college/indiana/2015/02/
26/college-athletes-continue-face-social-media-perils/24054307/

ESPN: The Social Science of Recruiting
http://www.espn.com/college-football/recruiting/story/_/id/
14646545/social-media-becomes-powerful-aide-dangerous-connection-
recruiting

The Guardian: Young Women on Instagram & Self-Esteem
https://www.theguardian.com/media/2015/nov/04/instagram-
young-women-self-esteem-essena-oneill

USA TODAY: Sextortion & Teens
https://www.usatoday.com/story/news/nation/2014/07/01/
sextortion-teens-online/11580633/

Rise & Stand: What's Illegal & What Isn't in Cyberbullying
http://www.riseandstand.net/whats-illegal-and-whats-not-when-it-
comes-to-cyber-harassment/

Computer Fraud & Abuse Act

https://ilt.eff.org/index.php/
Computer_Fraud_and_Abuse_Act_(CFAA)

Wired: Teens Sues over Cyberbullying
https://www.wired.com/2012/04/teen-sues-over-bullying/

Wired: The Story of Lori Drew
https://www.wired.com/2008/11/defendants-daug/

The Atlantic: What the Law Can't Do About Online Harassment
https://www.theatlantic.com/technology/archive/2014/11/what-
the-law-can-and-cant-do-about-online-harassment/382638/

Cyberbully Hotline: What is Catfishing?
http://www.cyberbullyhotline.com/catfishing.html

USA TODAY: Manti Teo's Catfish Story is a Common One
https://www.usatoday.com/story/sports/ncaaf/2013/01/17/manti-
teos-catfish-story-common/1566438/

Harpers: Mark Twain
https://harpers.org/author/marktwain/

US Magazine: Curt Schilling Hunts Down Guys Harassing His
Daughter
http://www.usmagazine.com/celebrity-news/news/curt-schilling-
tracks-down-guys-who-harassed-daughter-on-twitter-
201533#ixzz3TL8rqWbp

Reddit/People Magazine: Twenty People Who Lost Their Jobs Due to
Social Media
http://people.com/celebrity/employees-who-were-fired-because-of-
social-media-posts/

Huffington Post: Divorce & Social Media

http://www.huffingtonpost.com/2015/04/30/way-to-ruin-marriages-facebook_n_7183296.html

Stay Safe Online
https://staysafeonline.org/

Chapter 20: Date Rape, Teen Boys & Porn

American Girls: Social Media and the Secret Lives of Teenagers
Random House Audio Assets ©2016
ISBN:0553399217 9780553399219

The Atlantic
What We Knew About Date Rape Then, and What We Know Now
https://www.theatlantic.com/ideas/archive/2018/09/what-surveys-dating-back-decades-reveal-about-date-rape/571330/

WMBFNEWS
Man Attempts to Purchase Date Rape Drugs
https://www.wmbfnews.com/2019/06/17/man-attempts-purchase-date-rape-drugs-undercover-officer-report-says/

Chapter 21: Social Media & Teen Mental Health

Translational Psychiatry: Sex Differences in Depression
http://www.nature.com/tp/journal/v7/n5/full/tp2017105a.html?foxtrotcallback=true

Child-Mind Institute
https://childmind.org/

Time Magazine: Why the Kids Are Not Alright
http://time.com/magazine/us/4547305/november-7th-2016-vol-188-no-19-u-s/

Live Science: Will Tech Bring Humanity Together or Tear it Apart?
https://www.livescience.com/51392-will-tech-bring-humanity-together-or-tear-it-apart.html

The Human Memory
http://www.human-memory.net/brain_neurons.html

Depression & Suicide
https://theworldunplugged.wordpress.com/

Suicide Rates in Palo-Alto
http://www.mercurynews.com/2017/03/03/cdc-report-youth-suicide-rates-in-county-highest-in-palo-alto-morgan-hill/

Philly.com: Does Live Streaming Suicides Influence Our Kids?
http://www.philly.com/philly/health/kids-families/Livestream-suicides-Does-it-influence-our-kids.html

CDC: Suicide Contagion
https://www.cdc.gov/mmwr/preview/mmwrhtml/00031539.htm

TV Series: Thirteen Reasons Why
https://en.wikipedia.org/wiki/13_Reasons_Why

Baltimore Sun: Teens Turns to Social Media For Attention – Even Death
http://www.baltimoresun.com/news/opinion/oped/bs-ed-op-0619-social-media-suicide-20170615-story.html

Twisted Bard: Cyberbullyings Newest Frontier
http://www.twistedbard.com/cyberbullyings-newest-frontier/

Cyberbullying Research Center
https://cyberbullying.org/research.php

Chapter 22: The Role of Faith

https://www.americamagazine.org/faith/2019/08/19/science-faith-can-be-effective-against-adolescent-depression

https://www.icpsr.umich.edu/icpsrweb/DSDR/studies/21600

https://www.ncbi.nlm.nih.gov/books/NBK361016/

Chapter 23: Managing Your Child's Online Activity

McAfee: Cyberbullying Triple
https://www.mcafee.com/us/about/news/2014/q2/20140603-01.aspx

Huffington Post: Divorce & Social Media
http://www.huffingtonpost.com/2013/06/06/facebook-divorce-linked-i_n_3399727.html

Recover
https://recover.org/

Mashable: Seven Apps to Hide Your Sexy Photos
http://mashable.com/2014/09/29/sexting-photo-apps/#Nj5my..e1Pqi

uKnowKids
https://support.uknowkids.com/hc/en-us

ParentKit For OIS
https://parentkit.co/

OpenDNS
www.Opendns.com

Circle with Disney & Circle Go
https://meetcircle.com/

Luma
https://lumahome.com/

Torch
www.mytorch.com

Wall Street Journal: What They Know
http://www.wsj.com/public/page/what-they-know-digital-privacy.html

Raconteur: Where Did My Data Go?
https://www.raconteur.net/technology/where-does-my-data-go

The Guardian: Speak with Your Child About Online Safety
https://www.theguardian.com/technology/2014/aug/11/how-to-keep-kids-safe-online-children-advice

Elite Daily: Why You Should Never Take Another Naked Picture
http://elitedaily.com/women/taking-a-selfie-pic-nudie/737323/

The Telegraph: Sexting Myths Busted
http://www.telegraph.co.uk/women/womens-health/10985660/Sexting-scare-6-sexting-myths-busted.html

Ray Bradbury
https://www.biography.com/people/ray-bradbury-9223240

About the Author

Thanks for taking the time to read my book, Social Media & The Adolescent Digital Tribe: Navigating the Teen World State.

I'd like to tell you a little about myself. First and foremost, I am a father of two wonderful married daughters, a husband to my incredible wife Mary Beth and a grandfather to five beautiful grandchildren.

But I'm also a son, brother, uncle, father-in-law, son-in-law, former coach and teacher.

As you can see, family and education are my top priorities in life.

However, it is through my experiences in life and education that have allowed me the opportunity to understand the value that technology brings to our lives — as well as the challenges of managing these tools within a framework of families and schools. My experiences over the past thirty years have been exciting.

I started my career as a high school teacher and coach. I later worked at NCR Corporation in Dayton, Ohio for six years as writer and director of video-based and interactive programs related to the computer industry. I worked in the video and film production business for about twenty years before joining the IT Consulting industry in 1999.I have a Bachelor of Fine Arts Degree from the University of Cincinnati's Design, Art, Architecture & Planning program, a Masters Degree in Education & Communication from Xavier University, Executive Certification in Leadership & Management from The University of Notre Dame and a Masters Certificate and Executive Certification in Internet Marketing, University of San Francisco.

Acknowledgments

Many people need to be acknowledged in the development of this book. First and foremost is my wonderful wife Mary Beth who has been the glue to keep our presentations scheduled while also allowing me the time to write.

I want to acknowledge the many students, teachers, counselors, psychologists, psychiatrists, nurses, pediatricians, principals and school resource officers that have worked with me over the past ten years in helping families understand how social media can impact the lives of our youth.

Without their help, this book would not be possible.

However, I also want to thank the many prosecutors that have worked with me in a seven-county area in Ohio, Indiana and Kentucky. Many times, these fine people worked extra hours presenting to schools—only to then drive back to their offices to complete their already busy work days.

In particular, I want to thank Rob Sanders for taking time to speak with me about legal issues regarding teens and social media.

Additionally, a special thanks to Steve Franzen, Kentucky's Campbell County Attorney and, Dotty Smith, Chief Assistant Prosecutor, Municipal/Juvenile Divisions of the Clermont County

Prosecutor's Office. Steve and Dotty took the time to review their past cases so I could include real-life legal experiences with teens that had misused technology. Their help, professionalism and kindness are greatly appreciated.

Last, but not least, I need to thank my editor Annie Jenkinson at www.just-copyeditors.com for her work in editing this book so that my message was succinct and relevant to the readers. I'm sure she tore her hair out correcting my grammar and thought process.